Martini Lutheri fraudes damnarunt Christiæ
Lupus vorauit oues. REX Catholicus regnat vnus.
Misus DVX ALVA spes nostra, Alleluia.

De Tweedracht Verbeeld

*Prentkunst als propaganda
aan het begin
van de Tachtigjarige Oorlog*

Images of Discord

A graphic interpretation of the opening decades of the Eighty Years' War

James Tanis

Daniel Horst

BRYN MAWR COLLEGE LIBRARY

WILLIAM B. EERDMANS ✦ Grand Rapids

Copyright © 1993 Bryn Mawr College Library
101 North Merion Avenue
Bryn Mawr, Pennsylvania 19010-2899

PRINTED IN THE UNITED STATES OF AMERICA

By special arrangement with Bryn Mawr College,
Images of Discord: De Tweedracht Verbeeld is distributed by
Wm. B. Eerdmans Publishing Company, Grand Rapids, Michigan.

Images on the front cover, the half-title, and the title page are details
from Joris Hoefnagel's *An Allegory of the Spanish Tyranny* (number 10,
pages 56–57, Bryn Mawr College Library); the print on the back cover
is Willem Jacobszoon Delff's *The Throne of the Duke of Alva*, published by
Jan Petersz van de Venne (number 12, Atlas Van Stolk).

LIBRARY OF CONGRESS CATALOG CARD NUMBER 93-73325

ISBN 0-8028-0742-9

Contents

Preface

ON A PLEASANT AUTUMN EVENING, a dozen years ago, a group of Dutch-minded Pennsylvania friends gathered for dinner and conversation. Following dinner, one of the guests unrolled a large enigmatic Netherlandish allegorical print on the living room floor. At once a host of intriguing questions were raised. Though puzzling in many aspects, there were familiar elements in the print: for example, seventeen figures in chains were known to represent the seventeen Netherlandish provinces; the bearded two-faced image on the throne was that of the Spanish Duke of Alva, sent to The Netherlands by King Philip II of Spain to subdue his unruly northern subjects. But there were far more beguiling unfamiliar elements. Though no one could have realized it at that time, this book was, in fact, already beginning to take shape.

The print, now "NR 10" in this work, is dated 1570 and cryptically signed by a lower-case "a." It is a large etching, 41 by 96 centimeters, printed on three attached sheets—possibly the earliest Netherlandish etching of such dimensions. Though numbers marking the multitudinous figures have been rubbed off in places, numbers enough remain to indicate that at least eighty-five elements had at one time been identified in a now missing key.

The owner, Harlan J. Berk of Chicago, had forwarded the print to Netherlandish art historian Ellen Jacobowitz, now at the Cranbrook Institute of Science. Ellen was the dinner guest who shared the etching with her eager companions. Following the first evening's discussion of the work, Harlan Berk lent it to Bryn Mawr College Library for study. Later he most generously gave the etching to the College for its growing collection of works of art on paper. We feel that he has been twice wise: first in spotting the print in a London shop and second in placing it permanently at the College Library. A decade of research, both in the United States and Europe, has led to an unraveling of many of the historical, allegorical, and emblematical enigmas.

Research was initially shared by Dutch scholars Robert J. Zijp, formerly of Utrecht's Rijksmuseum Het Catharijneconvent; Carl Nix, curator of Rotterdam's Stichting Atlas Van Stolk; and Daniel Horst of the Rijksprentenkabinet in Amsterdam's Rijksmuseum. Variously helpful in many of the identifications, they also pointed to other relevant prints and drawings. A suggestion from Professor Karel Porteman of the Katholieke Universiteit Leuven (Louvain) proved a critical step in identifying monogrammist "a" as the artist Joris Hoefnagel of Antwerp. Professor Porteman has also been most helpful in refining the translations of the sixteenth-century texts. Several other scholars and a host of prints, books, and articles have shed increasing light on the *Allegory* and thereby helped to create *Images of Discord*.

Images first began to take shape at Atlas Van Stolk, when print after print was examined for possible ties to Hoefnagel's *Allegory*. From the start Carl Nix's interest and helpfulness made Atlas Van Stolk the ideal research base for the undertaking. Equally logical, therefore, was the choice of Atlas Van Stolk as the site of the exhibition first bringing the print to the notice of those tantalized by art, propaganda, and politics, as well as those primarily interested in Netherlandish history.

Exhibitions follow at the Katholieke Universiteitsbibliotheek, Leuven; the Philadelphia Museum of Art; and the Museum of the University of Indiana, Bloomington. We are most appreciative of the interest and cooperation of the directors of the several museums: Drs Jan Roegiers, Ann d'Harnoncourt, and Adelheid M. Gealt. In the overall planning, the expertise of Philadelphia Museum's Suzanne F. Wells and Innis Shoemaker greatly facilitated the effort. From the outset Lawrence W. Nichols, formerly of the Philadelphia Museum, encouraged and promoted the project, sharing his own deep understanding of Netherlandish art.

A fortuitous happening brought Daniel Horst into the project. While working on his *doctoraalscriptie* on caricatures of Alva (*Spotprenten op Alva*), he learned through Robert Zijp of the existence of Bryn Mawr's print. From that point on his involvement followed as natural consequence, and his full participation in planning and writing this book has greatly enlarged its breadth and scholarly usefulness.

Few of the prints discussed in this volume bear established titles. Most titles vary from citation to citation. In those few cases where a title is part of the text of the print itself, that original title is given in parentheses beneath its English translation. Other titles have been derived from traditional nomenclature, while at the same time an attempt has been made to generate distinctive names. The anonymity of many of the artists has further complicated the study, but many of the prints produced within the boundaries of the Low Countries were clandestinely published in order to save the artist and printer from the hangman's noose.

The "Literature" notes in the catalog entries include citations in the basic reference works for early Netherlandish historical prints. Also included is *Ketters en Papen*, the most helpfully detailed exhibition catalog. The following abbreviations are used:

F.M.   =   Muller, F., *De Nederlandsche Geschiedenis in platen.*
F.M.S.   =   Muller *Supplement.*
F.M.-RPK =   Rijksprentenkabinet additions to Muller.
A.V.S.   =   Rijn, G. van, *Atlas Van Stolk, Katalogus.*
Hollstein   =   Hollstein, F. W. H., *Dutch and Flemish Etchings.*
K. en P.   =   *Ketters en Papen onder Filips II.*

Also included are citations to other books and articles specifically related to the particular catalog entry. The *Bibliography* includes those works most used in writing the essays and preparing the catalog entries. For general background, emphasis has been placed on English language volumes, since extensive guides to Dutch works are more readily available.

We are most appreciative of the generous cooperation of those institutions lending materials for the exhibitions which coincide with the publication of this volume: the Rijksprentenkabinet of the Rijksmuseum, Amsterdam; the Prentenkabinet of the Koninklijke Bibliotheek Albert I, Brussels; Bryn Mawr College Library, Bryn Mawr, Pennsylvania; Museum Mr Simon van Gijn, Dordrecht; Penningkabinet der Rijksuniversiteit, Leiden; Department of Prints and Drawings, Metropolitan Museum of Art, New York; Bibliothèque Nationale, Paris; Stichting Atlas Van Stolk, Historisch Museum Rotterdam; Bibliothèque Municipale, Rouen; and the Rijksmuseum Het Catharijneconvent, Utrecht. For the loan of Frans Hogenberg's *Leo Belgicus* map, we are indebted to Mr and Mrs Norman R. Bobins.

In addition to the lending institutions, we are indebted to the following institutions for providing photographs and permission to publish works in their collections: Andover-Harvard Theological Library, Harvard Divinity School, Cambridge, Massachusetts (NR XI); The Folger Shakespeare Library, Washington, District of Columbia (NR XL); Fundación Casa de Alba, Madrid (NR XXXVI); Hamburger Kunsthalle, Hamburg (NR III); Herzog August Bibliothek, Wolfenbuttel (NR XXXI); Prentenkabinet der Rijksuniversiteit, Leiden (nr xxxii); and Museum Boymans-van Beuningen, Rotterdam (NR XXXV).

The interest and support of Daniel and Joanna Semel Rose have been enabling from the outset of this undertaking and critical to the production of this volume. For further assistance in helping make possible this book and the accompanying exhibition, we are grateful to Mr and Mrs W. Graham Arader III, Reginald and Lois Collier, Irene Tanis Keigler, Julie McGee, The Netherlands Society of Philadelphia, Katherine K. Roosenburg, and other anonymous donors. Book cover and poster designs were created by Jack Freas. Initial secretarial help was contributed by Ann Gross. Maps were drawn by Kathryn M. Yanity.

In The Netherlands the assistance and participation of Sanne Jolles and Jan H. Waszink have been particularly valuable.

This project would not have been possible without the continuing support of Bryn Mawr College, its President, Mary Patterson McPherson, and the staff of Bryn Mawr College Library. The ramifications of this undertaking have involved almost everyone in some interesting way or other. Pho-

tographic assistance was provided by Karl Dimler and David Sullivan. In the Director's Office John Dooley provided editorial service, Lee O'Leary typing assistance, and Mary Devlin unstinting secretarial service well beyond all expectation. Mary Leahy contributed collegially at every phase of planning and implementation.

Increasingly the interrelationship of history and history of art has been recognized as an unplumbed source for humanistic research. The works of art in this book document not only political history, but also religious, economic, and social history. They are compositions of broad appeal— prints designed to stimulate intellectual curiosity. We are most grateful for the international cooperation evinced by the seventeen supporting institutions, confirming the intentions and assuring the results of this undertaking.

My wife, Flossie, has been part of this project since the evening the *Allegory* was first unrolled. No step in the long process (except this last paragraph) escaped her caring eye. Much of the inevitable fall-out landed on her patient shoulders. To her this work is *van harte* dedicated.

JAMES TANIS
Professor of History and
The Constance A. Jones Director of Libraries
Bryn Mawr College

ix

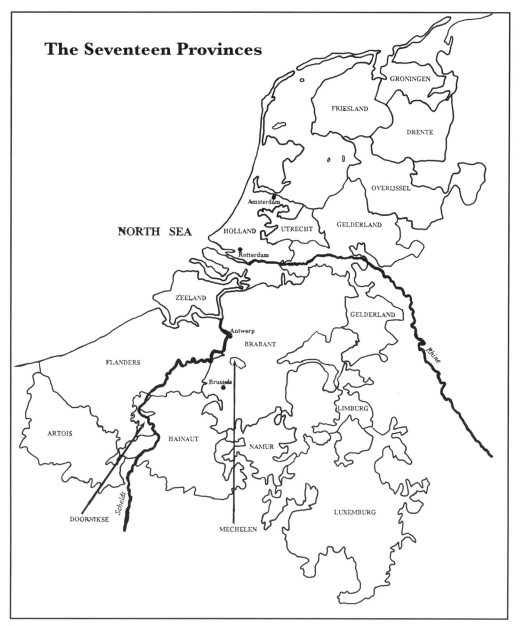

The Seventeen Provinces

GRONINGEN

FRIESLAND

DRENTE

OVERIJSSEL

Amsterdam

NORTH SEA

HOLLAND   UTRECHT   GELDERLAND

Rotterdam

ZEELAND

GELDERLAND

Antwerp

BRABANT

Rhine

FLANDERS

Brussels

LIMBURG

ARTOIS

HAINAUT   NAMUR

Scheldt

LUXEMBURG

DOORNIKSE

MECHELEN

THE SEVENTEEN PROVINCES
The geographical areas denoted on this outline map as the Seventeen Provinces represent one stage in a fluctuating boundary situation. The word "province" was used to describe a variety of geo-political divisions including counties, dukedoms, a bishopric, and a seigniory.

THE NETHERLANDISH LION LEO BELGICUS I
Designed about 1579 by Michael Aitzinger, this first *Leo Belgicus* map was engraved by Frans Hogenberg, who added the seventeen provincial coats-of-arms. Symbolizing the power and bravery of The Netherlands, this innovative cartographic image was frequently reprinted, modified, and reissued.

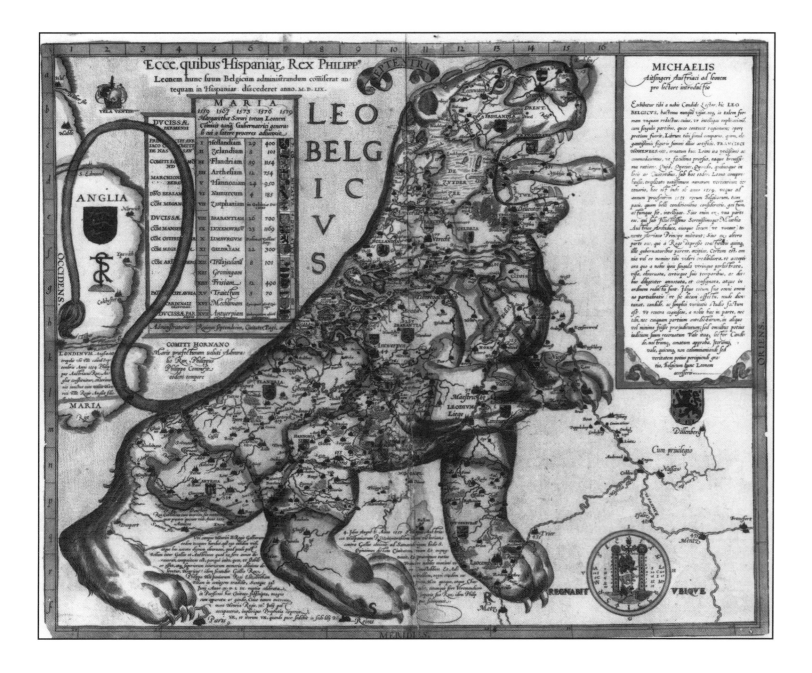

I

Background: Prints, Propaganda, & Politics

In the early mornng hours of 5 June 1568 a scaffold was constructed on the market place in Brussels. Two stakes with spearpoints were affixed. An altar with a silver crucifix was erected upon it. Twenty-two companies of Spanish soldiers took their places among the gathering crowds. On order of the Duke of Alva, and some said signed by King Philip II, the Counts of Egmond and Hoorne were to be executed on charges they declared false and on which they professed their innocence.

At ten o'clock Egmond was led up the stairs of the scaffold. He asked if there might be grace. He was told there would be none. Laying aside his gold-lace-bordered black cape, he was the first to face the executioner's sword. Then Hoorne, after bidding the crowd good fortune, like Egmond, knelt and tendered his spirit to God. With one blow each, their lives ended. The executioner impaled their bloody heads on the spearpoints, where they remained for the next two hours. Even the Spanish soldiers were moved to tears. Weeping citizens dipped their handkerchiefs in the blood, saving them for personal memorials. All the land mourned the deaths of the two counts. Alva, who had thought to instill fear and obedience by this demonstration of force, instead brought on himself the hatred of the people. Even a half-century later, graphic figures of Egmond, Hoorne, and Alva were still the most emotional symbols of the struggle of The Netherlands against Spain, of freedom against tyranny.

The beginning of the Eighty Years' War in the Low Countries is traditionally marked by the executions of June 1568. The conflict, which began as a local struggle against Spanish authority, was to become worldwide, eventually extending to outposts in Asia and the Americas. When a peace conference was finally convened in German Münster in 1648, its concerns involved all the foremost European powers. Thus a seemingly contained event in the Southern Netherlands (present-day Belgium) escalated into a major international conflict, resulting in the originally-unintended independence of the Northern Netherlands (now The Netherlands.)

The conflict, begun over "rights and privileges," evolved into a struggle over "liberty and freedom." The printed word, invented little more than a hundred years before, had already become a powerful means of communication. The Eighty Years' War, however, was to become the first major conflict to be fought in any telling measure with paper propaganda. Pamphlets and broadsides were produced in great numbers. Most interesting of those were the ones with graphic images, created to stir the emotions and to win the support of the people. Prints, developed not much earlier than the printed word, were often wedded to text. So effective were these products during the first years of the struggle, that

I. Pope Paul II Contesting with Frederick III (Anonymous, ca 1470)

II. Pope Paul III Contesting with Charles V (Anonymous, image ca 1548)

Many were designed to replace the illuminations found in manuscript texts and to illustrate the newly-developed books printed from type. Others were issued on single sheets for decorative or devotional use. Like evolving media before and since, they were also adapted to social and political ends.

Much of the work for popular presses was unsigned by the artists. Borrowing from one print to create another became a standard procedure, when the largely anonymous artists adapted ideas from a growing pool of images. One such image was the gaping Mouth of Hell. It appeared frequently in medieval portrayals of the Last Judgement; it reappeared in several of the religio-political works related to and included in this study.

In addition to giving form to new artistic imaginings, artists at times simply retitled old scenarios, renaming figures in earlier works with updated identities. For example, a popular 1470 woodcut illustrating the themes and symbols devised in the earliest prints became emblems for the war at each critical stage.

Already during the second half of the fifteenth century, prints created as illustrations became increasingly more popular in Northern Europe.

power struggle between Pope Paul II and Emperor Frederick III was copied by several woodcutters to meet wide demand of titillated viewers (NR I). Later a copy came into the hands of another anonymous artist who redrew it for an updated version of the print (NR II). Here the ship as the symbol of power is still the Church; *Leo Belgicus*, the lion on which the Emperor steadies one foot, still reflects the critical role of the Low Countries. The contesting *dramatis personae*, however, have changed. The Pope is now Paul III and the Emperor is Charles V.

As the above woodcut testifies, by the 1470s allegorical and emblematical embellishments in religious and political prints were found to be an effective means of communicating ideas. Printing made it comparatively simple and inexpensive to spread an image across the continent. The creation of ideological cartoons became an increasingly popular artistic venture, taking cues from the often amusing figures in the decorative borders imaginatively conceived by medieval illuminators. By the time of the Reformation, the genre of pictorial narrative was well established, and various techniques of printmaking were being exploited.

The Reformation, more than any previous series of happenings, gave increased impetus to the graphic image as an effective means of arousing broad popular interest. Though the theological issues of the Reformation have ancient roots, the beginning of the Reformation as event is usually chron-

icled from Martin Luther's posting of his Ninety-Five Theses in late October 1517. The next major public event was the Leipzig Disputation, held from 27 June through 16 July 1519. The initial disputants were the scholastic Professor Johann Eck of the University of Ingolstadt, who had written against Luther's Theses, and the evangelical Professor Andreas Bodenstein von Karlstadt of the University of Wittenberg. Midway through the dispute Karlstadt was joined by Luther. Already in the spring of 1519 Karlstadt had collaborated with his friend, the Wittenberg artist Lucas Cranach the Elder, in producing the *Fuhrwagen* (freightwagon), the first graphic of the Reformation (NR III). Ironically it was Karlstadt, two years later, who called for the destruction of religious images.

The *Fuhrwagen* gave visual form to Karlstadt's fundamental objection to the theological position represented by Eck. Karlstadt's embrace of Augustine's position on the bondage of the will is pictured in the upper half of the print. The pious layman in the cart pulled by eight horses is headed toward the risen crucified Christ, with Saints Augustine and Paul astride two of the horses. A demon attempts in vain to hold back the wagon by its wheel. The cart below carries a cleric, who shares the ride with another demon. The horses pull that wagon straight to the Mouth of Hell. There the damned join other demonic monsters in awaiting the erring cleric who defends the freedom

of the will and the blessedness of works' righteousness. Though there were no personal names attached to these figures, it did not take Eck very long to identify himself as the expostulating cleric headed for hell.

The wood block was cut with open spaces for the text to be inset. The first copies Karlstadt provided with hand-written Latin inscriptions. They were soon followed by an edition with printed Latin text (of which only a fragment remains) and then by the German edition (of which two known copies survive). In his accompanying pamphlet the Reformer noted his particular desire to reach the younger generation. It must have been a popular print, for traces of the *Fuhrwagen* are to be found in various contexts. A copy was delivered to artist Albrecht Dürer by his humanist friend Christoph Scheurl; another was sent by Eck with angry complaints to the Elector of Saxony; and students were asked their opinions of the print in the confessional, the better to correct their errors and assign appropriate penance for heretical thoughts. The artist Hans Sebald Beham reused the idea in an anti-Catholic woodcut of 1524. The *Fuhrwagen* was Cranach's first polemical woodcut, anticipating his better-known *Passional Christi und Antichristi* of 1521. In this latter more expansive series Cranach followed the same traditional didactic techniques he had employed in the *Fuhrwagen*, relying on the juxtaposition of good and evil, of Reformation and Rome (NR IV). These prints more than

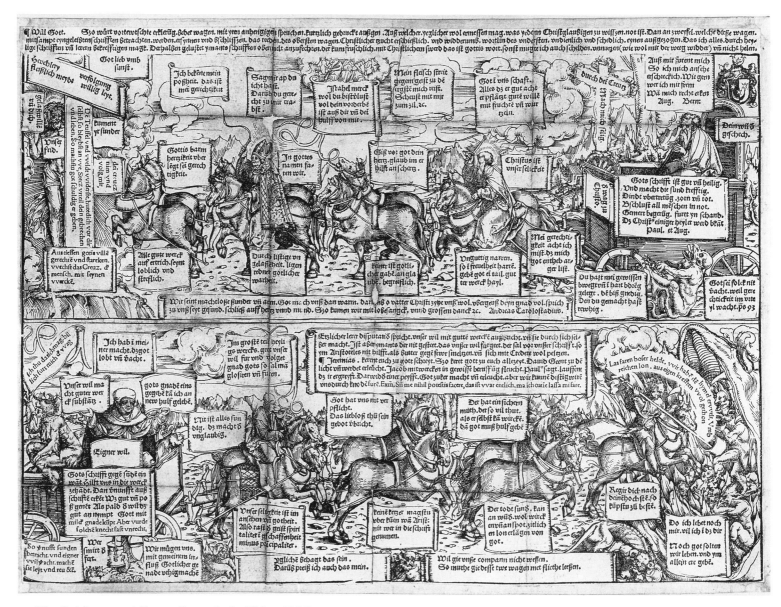

III. The freight-wagon (Lucas Cranach the Elder, 1519)

4

any others early established the effectiveness of the genre.

Catholic artists took up the medium as well. Most popular of their works was the woodcut, at one time attributed to Hans Brosamer, picturing an apocalyptic seven-headed Luther (NR V). It was designed to embellish the title-page of the theologian Johannes Cochlaeus' tract *Septiceps Lutherus* (The Seven-headed Luther), a work published in 1529 in both Latin and German. The intriguing image, drawn from the New Testament book of *The Revelation,* was also adapted by the Protestants, with a text by Hans Sachs and an anonymous woodcut of a seven-headed papal monster. Numerous other derivative prints followed on both sides of the ongoing dispute, as reflected in CATALOG NR 1. In such ways the use of prints gained a significant place in the ever-fecund hands of both the Catholic and Protestant propagandists.

The prints and texts of the Reformation early found their way into The Netherlands. Charles V's fierce suppression of new religious ideas in the Burgundian Netherlands made the open circulation of these works impossible and the clandestine circulation deadly dangerous. The same was true in the areas of northeastern Netherlands under the rule of the passionately anti-heretical Karel van Gelder. Remnants from these early years are thus rare indeed.

One of the most telling survivals is a satirical drawing of the Catholic Church's

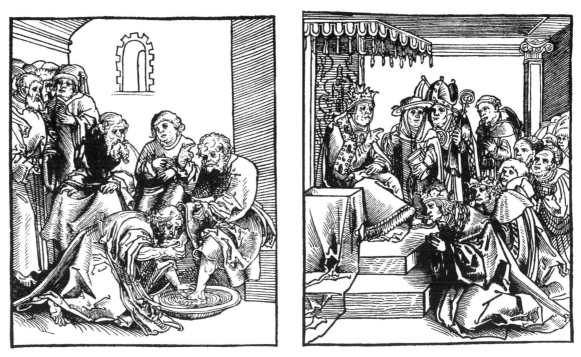

IV. Christ and the Antichrist (Lucas Cranach the Elder, 1521)

misuse of power, attributed to the Brussels workshop of Barent van Orley, dating from about 1526 (NR VI). Barent was born into a family of artists. In 1515 he was appointed official court painter by Margaretha of Austria, Regent of The Netherlands and aunt of Charles V. Barent's designs for tapestries and stained glass windows were especially prized. In 1527 Barent, his family, his father Valentin and brother Everard were among a group of artists and craftspersons arrested for participating in clandestine Protestant meetings. Though spared more serious punishment by the intervention of the regent Margaretha, the accused were sentenced to fines and work for the Brussels Church of Saint Gudule. From this circle of artists came this drawing, entitled *De contemptu mundi* (Concerning Contempt for the World). Possibly, it was itself a copy of a painting. It appears to have been drawn for reproduction as a woodcut, and in that respect is typical of other products of Barent's workshop. Letters of the alphabet on the drawing keyed the complex images to a now-missing text. A viewer should begin reading the work in the upper left-hand corner, where Christ appears on a globe holding the scales of the Last Judgement, *Justitia et Judicium*. The theme of divine judgement, which appears here emblematically, is found in many of the prints later in the century. The Mouth of Hell, surmounted by the Whore of Babylon wearing a papal tiara, fills the lower right-hand cor-

ner. The idea may have been borrowed from the 1508 title-page of Eloy d'Amerval's tract, *Livre de la diablerie* (NR VII) or from a similar work. Because of the subversive nature of the drawing, it was probably hidden away for private viewing only, and so survived.

Later in the century the image was indeed engraved, possibly in the late 1550s. The text appended to CATALOG NR 6 may preserve the content of the drawing's missing text. The lengthy description beneath the print notes that due to the work of the Devil "we are separated from Christ's word and led to damnation." Then the anonymous author adds: "Such appears clearly through this figure, which God has wonderfully preserved. Ordered by an abbot, painted and then copied. And so to this hour it openly remains in the Roman Empire. At Luik in a powerful bishop's city." It is not clear from the text whether "ordering" implied that the abbot simply commissioned the work or that he created its program—or some combination of the two. Also, the word *schilderen* (which originally meant to decorate a shield and which later came unambiguously to mean "painted") could in sixteenth-century parlance also mean "draw a picture." The drawing and the print have been intriguingly discussed by Karel G. Boon in his preface to the catalog of *The Netherlandish and German Drawings of the XVth and XVIth Centuries* in the Frits Lugt Collection.

v. The Seven-headed Luther (Anonymous, 1529)

VI. Concerning Contempt for the World (School of van Orley, ca 1526)

By 1570 a copy of the print (presumably) had fallen into the hands of the Antwerp artist Joris Hoefnagel. There it served as a major source for the imagery of his allegory on the Spanish suppression of The Netherlands (CATALOG NR 10) and so became a major link in this study. In differing ways the *De contemptu mundi* print and Hoefnagel's *Allegory* give testimony to the continuing power of graphic images. In some instances the figures themselves were simply reused; for example, the demon with the bellows and the Whore of Babylon are perched similarly in both prints on the head of the Mouth of Hell. In other instances, images were altered when reused by Hoefnagel, as in the case of the mini-monster holding a mirror to the historical parade across the bottom of *De contemptu mundi*. On the right-hand side in Hoefnagel's print, the artist himself holds the mirror to the broad historical pageant.

Allegorical and emblematic images had grown in popularity in Europe since Milan-

7

ese lawyer Andrea Alciati's *Emblematum liber* first appeared in Augsburg in 1531. Of the humanist Alciati, Erasmus wrote that he was the most jurisprudent of orators and the most eloquent of lawyers. From those diverse talents came the formulation and publication of the first pure emblem book. A true emblem was conceived of in three parts: a motto, an image or illustration, and an explication. (See NR XXVII.)

It was not until 1554 that the first emblem book was printed in the Low Countries. The volume, a work in Dutch, was published by a woman, known as the widow of the publisher Jacob van Liesveldt. By that time Latin, French, and German volumes were already long popular throughout the region. International book trade was a mark of the times, and the learned community was as comfortable with a Latin text as it was with a vernacular one. Though emblem books often employed the same figure for two or more different meanings, nonetheless they provided a common vocabulary for artist and writer alike.

By 1560 loose sheet prints with allegorical programs were also gaining in popularity, particularly those with designs by Pieter Bruegel the Elder. Bruegel, already established as a landscape artist, began designing his satirical prints in 1556. First he drew on the popular

VII. The Mouth of Hell (Anonymous, 1508)

style of the late fifteenth-century artist Hieronymous Bosch, but by the time his widely admired series of the Seven Deadly Sins appeared in 1558, his own reputation in this genre was established.

Bruegel reinterpreted the late Gothic Netherlandish tradition in a new mode, using, for example, small calendar images from Books of Hours to inspire his studies of the "Months" and of "Children's Games." Proverbs, first firmly established in the Netherlandish literary tradition by Erasmus, were drawn in variety by Bruegel. Eagerly purchased prints were engraved and etched after his designs by a number of different artists. Already in 1556 he depicted the proverb *The Ass in School (De Ezel op School)* for an engraving to follow in 1557 (NR VIII). "Even if the ass goes to school to learn, he remains an ass and won't return a horse."

Bruegel's images have been variously interpreted. Many scholars have found hidden references to political and religious events of his day. Are Herod's forces, pictured in the painting *Massacre of the Innocents*, led by the Duke of Alva? And what other subtle allusions did Netherlanders find in his works? Born sometime between 1525 and 1530, Bruegel died in 1569, a comparatively young man. Yet he left a legacy of meaning in imagery, color, and design that delighted his countrymen and significantly influenced Netherlandish artists for the century to follow—and among those artists was the little-known Joris Hoefnagel.

PARISIOS STOLIDVM SI QVIS TRANSMITTAT ASELLVM·SI HIC EST ASINVS NON ERIT ILLIC EQVVS·
Al rejst den efele ter scholen om leeren / ift eenen efele hij en fal gheen peert weder keeren

VIII. The Ass in School (Pieter Bruegel the Elder, 1556)

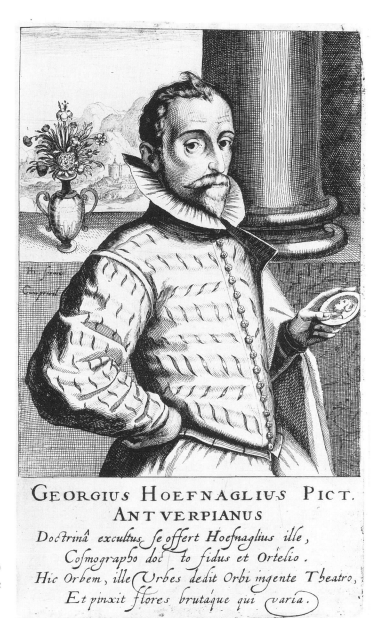

GEORGIUS HOEFNAGLIUS PICT.
ANTVERPIANUS

Doctrinâ excultus se offert Hoefnaglius ille,
    Cosmographo doc to fidus et Ortelio.
Hic Orbem, ille Urbes dedit Orbi ingente Theatro,
    Et pinxit flores brutáque qui varia.

JORIS HOEFNAGEL
Portrait by Hendrik Hondius I, 1573–1650
Engraving from *Pictorum aliquot celebrium praecipuae Germaniae Inferioris effigies.*
The Hague, 1610, part II, nr 47.

II

Joris Hoefnagel & the Revolt of The Netherlands

THE DUKE OF ALVA would eagerly have included the head of Prince Willem of Orange on the spikes in the Brussels market place, could his men have laid their hands on him. Acknowledged leader by default of an undeclared revolt, Willem had managed his escape from territories under Alva's control. In reprisal, his son Philips Willem was captured and sent to Spain. Father and son were not to meet again. Willem was a man of the court, adept in courtly ways and wise to the politics of international intrigue. He would as gladly have eschewed the latter, as he embraced the former, but the times gave him no choice.

Like his contemporary Willem the Silent, the artist Joris Hoefnagel was a man of broad humanist sympathies. Though both were caught up in the religio-political events of the late 1560s, both would gladly have retained their freer social roles. Willem was never to escape from his involvement; indeed it was to cost him his life. Joris, to a large degree, was later able to relocate, refocus his interests, and reshape his enterprises. For both, however, 1570 was a milestone year of intense political entanglement. It is not known if their paths crossed literally; Willem, about nine years Joris's elder, was ostensibly on a higher rung of the social ladder. The Prince of Orange did directly enter Joris's artistic world, however, when his etched figure was shown fleeing The Netherlands for his ancestral German home, as seen in this detail from Hoefnagel's *Allegory of the Spanish Tyranny* (NR IX).

Joris, born in 1542 in a well-to-do Antwerp jewel-merchant family, indulged in wide-ranging travels. Such journeys provided him with opportunities to sketch sights and scenes which were later to become an invaluable part of the *Civitates Orbis Terrarum* (the first published atlas of the world's cities, produced by Georg Braun and Frans Hogenberg). In his early twenties Joris Hoefnagel seemed most at home in Spain,

IX. Willem Flees from The Netherlands (Hoefnagel, 1570)

CONSILIEN, DECRÉTEN, DECRETALEN, CLEMENTINE, EXTRAVAGANTES.

x. Alva in the Mouth of Hell (Hoefnagel, 1570)

Ongoing persecutions in The Netherlands, begun during the first years of the Reformation under the rule of Charles V, were continued even more zealously under Philip II. In fact, in order to effect this policy Philip sent the Iron Duke of Alva to The Netherlands, where he arrived in December 1567, near the time of Hoefnagel's return to Antwerp from Spain. As noted in the first essay, in June 1568, with the concurrence of the so-called Council of Blood, Alva had ordered the beheading of Willem's close friends, the Counts Egmond and Hoorne. Together with Philip II all had been members of the elite Order of the Knights of the Golden Fleece. Such violence against fellow members of the Order was virtually inconceivable. This dramatic event Joris also captured in his allegorical etching of the Spanish tyranny, a study he completed after his return from London to Antwerp in November 1570.

In his *Allegory* Hoefnagel depicts the Spanish Duke enthroned in the Mouth of Hell (NR X), much as an artist in the Cranach workshop had positioned the Pope as "Prince of Hell" in a Luther tract of 1545 (NR XI). Joris shows Alva and his entourage perched on a mighty volume of the Decretals of the Church, resting in turn on the heads of the powers supporting the Inquisition: the military arm, the spiritual arm, the theological arm, and the official religio-political arm. The whole configuration simulates a great stage setting.

where he visited extendedly from 1563 through1567. Then, after a short return to Antwerp, he traveled to London in early 1568. There he shared in the large Netherlandish community which carried on political and business activities within the safer confines of England's metropolis. The group was also enlarged from time to time by the influx of Protestant religious refugees.

How did Hoefnagel move from his earlier affectionate ties to Spain to the apparently anti-Spanish anti-ecclesiastical imagery of his allegory? The clues lie in part in his emblem book entitled *Patientia*, which he had drawn in England in 1569, the year before he etched the print. For the *Patientia* he had also written verses, some in Flemish, others in French, and yet others in Spanish.

XI. The Prince of Hell (School of Cranach, 1545)

The illustrated manuscript (now in the Library at Rouen) was dedicated to a close friend, the Dutch merchant Johannes Radermacher, who had gone to London to escape religious persecution in 1566. (In 1590, more than twenty years later, Hoefnagel was to dedicate to Radermacher an allegorical oil painting celebrating their long mutual friendship.) *Patientia* reflected the frustrations of the Lowlanders which Hoefnagel had witnessed in those few months between his arrival in Antwerp from Spain and his departure for England. Those feelings, simulated in the sketch entitled "Patient in Adversity," were reinforced by the stories of political and religious refugees who were constantly arriving in London (NR XII).

The twenty-four drawings are genre scenes, picturing life in small vignettes, with motto-like designations and explanatory epigrams in octaves below, giving political meaning to otherwise non-political views. Which of the emblems can be related to the Netherlandish scene is sometimes a matter of debate. (The drawings are in bistre, over pencil sketches.) Though all are

given emblematical meaning in the epigrams, only the drawing of *Patientia* herself is truly allegorical (NR XIII). Here she sits, her feet in stocks, being consoled by Hope.

I am Patience personified.
Hope consoles me in all my sufferings,
Hope, she cheers me in my sadness.
She lifts my heart towards heaven's tune.
…

You too should place your hope and
 consolation in the Lord;
Blessed is the person who builds on Him
 alone.

Willem the Silent had also counseled patience in adversity. Indeed his nickname "the Silent" did not reflect a lack of conversational gifts but a patient control of what to say and when to say it, but most importantly, what not to say.

Patientia was a favorite theme of sixteenth-century Netherlandish artists. Karel G. Boon discusses this idea in his article "*Patientia* dans les gravures de la Reforme aux Pays-Bas." One of the prints examined is Pieter Bruegel's complex *Patientia* engraving (NR XIV). Hoefnagel frequently revealed his familiarity with Bruegel's idioms; nevertheless an earlier suggestion that he studied with Bruegel has not been supported. (Hoefnagel claimed to be self-taught, though Karel van Mander asserted that he had studied with Hans Bol. He almost certainly had some instruction from others as well.)

XII. Patient in Adversity (Hoefnagel, 1569)

XIII. Patience (Hoefnagel, 1569)

PATIENTIA

H·Cock·excude·1557.   P·   Brueghel·Inuent·
                                                       ME.

PATIENTIA EST MALORVM QVÆ AVT INFERVNTVR, AVT ACCIDVNT, CVM ÆQVANIMITATE PERLATIO Lact·Inst·Lib·5.

xiv. Patience (Pieter Bruegel the Elder, 1557)

That the map maker Abraham Ortelius was a very close friend of both Bruegel and Hoefnagel is also of significance. All three were captivated by emblematics and enriched their respective artistic endeavors with imaginative conceits.

Several of the album's emblems are self-revealing of Joris, placing him or his alter ego in the drawing itself. This he also does in the allegorical print, where he holds up a mirror to the scene he portrays (NR XV). Engendering other personal questions is this drawing of a man (NR XVI), presumably leaving Spain and wearing a sanbenito, the yellow penitential garment with a red St Andrew's cross in which heretics were forced to dress as a sign of infamy. The Patient Sanbenitado muses:

> Reflect on me, all you who trade in
>   Spanish lands.
> It is the Inquisition.
> In this manner the holy office outfits them.
> They humiliate those who do not rule their
>   tongues well,
> And bring into want many fine persons
> With no opportunity for complaints.
> The sanbenito you must wear for it.
> "Mouth closed, Purse closed." That is the
>   world's device.

One wonders if Hoefnagel himself had run afoul of the Inquisition before leaving Spain. Many evidences, however, support the supposition that he was not an ardent

xv. Self-portrait with a Mirror (Hoefnagel, 1570)

Protestant, and perhaps not, strictly speaking, a Protestant at all. Several family members, nonetheless, were affiliated with *The Family of Love*, a loosely gathered fellowship of intellectuals holding deep spiritual concerns but placing little importance on the visible church—Protestant or Catholic. In 1570 Willem the Silent was also far from asserting his later Protestant affirmations. Like Bruegel, Hoefnagel seems to have been deeply marked by Neo-Stoicism, and his personal faith was probably much closer to the Christian humanism of his day than to either the Catholicism of the Roman Catholic Church or the Calvinism of the growing Flemish Reformation. Yet in another emblem (NR XVII) he seems to assert his belief that one must not stand apart from the tragic events of the times. He entitles it "The Patient Horned One."

> Patient horned one they call me,
>   Seeing there what I have no desire to see;
> Finding another with my wife,
> I consent by my closed mouth
> O what dishonor grows out of me,
> What humiliation. I stop the complaining
> And turn over the page.
> Who acts thus, deserves such a reward.

"The Patient Captive" (NR XVIII) pictures a Christian merchant captured by a Turk. It may simultaneously provide an allegory of the plight of The Netherlands under Alva.

Unholy the hour in which I was born,
Unholier the day of tribulation
Which comes upon me in a foreign nation.
Almighty God, turn away your anger.
Earlier I had what now I have lost,
My goods, my money, friends, and
    relatives.

Misery now must end my days.
Little does one know whereto one is born.

Two of Hoefnagel's drawings turn on the plight of the Spanish soldiers, describing their misery in an attempt to instruct his readers on the folly of war. They also help

clarify his continuing affection for the Spanish people, as he turned his animus towards the powers of Spanish rule. In one (NR XIX), two wounded soldiers are struggling to help one another along. The one remarks, "My brother, what must we do?" The other replies, "Folks could say to us, 'Who seeks war

XVI. The Patient Sanbenitado (Hoefnagel, 1569)

XVII. The Patient Horned One (Hoefnagel, 1569)

XVIII. The Patient Captive (Hoefnagel, 1569)

in foreign lands, seeks misery.' It is our fault; let us not seek further." The other is entitled "The Patient Dupe" (NR XX).

Our Blessed Lady, serve me as guide.
I swear by God that I meant to go
To the golden world, journeying to
    Flanders.
Truly, it is rather frozen, one could say.
I was disillusioned by cold, by hunger.
O what deceit.
Spain, Spain, if only I had not left you.
Who seeks the unknown,
Should not complain over what he has
    lost.

Early in the booklet (NR XXI) "Patient Community" asks, "What must the poor community suffer, if the princes desire to go to war?" The emblem shows a flock of sheep about to be shorn. Another (NR XXII) is titled "Patient Merchant."

We merchants are in a bad way.
We bring princes and lands to
    prosperity.
Our trade brings prosperity
    everywhere.
Now they come and confiscate our
    goods,
Even ransom our persons.
Through war, controversy, or such
    quarrels,
Have Patience, the Lord will reward us.
God gives, God takes, 'tis all the Lord's
    will.

What might seem Calvinistic in this last octave is more clearly stoic, when one reflects on the context.

XIX. Patient Soldiers (Hoefnagel, 1569)

XX. The Patient Dupe (Hoefnagel, 1569)

One additional emblem shows two men (NR XXIII), a winner and a loser, playing backgammon. The game is emblematic of life in the troubled world; the caged bird represents the plight of the Netherlanders; and the picture of Saint George (in Dutch *Sint Joris*) is emblematic of the artist himself.

18

In his extraordinarily large allegorical *historieprent*, dated 1570, Hoefnagel signed himself with a lower-case "a" enclosed in a diamond, mounted on a milestone. The diamond was symbolic of the family's eminence as jewel merchants; the "a" presumably reflected his birthplace, standing for his frequently used latinized cognomen Georgius Hoefnaglius Antwerpianus (NR XXIV). When Hoefnagel returned to Antwerp in the fall of 1570, the Netherlandish Revolt was still undefined; little could he

XXIII. The Patient Backgammon Player (Hoefnagel, 1569)

XXI. The Patient Community (Hoefnagel, 1569)

XXII. The Patient Merchant (Hoefnagel, 1569)

19

have imagined that the war already in its third year would become an Eighty Years' War. The Revolt was still largely confined to the Southern Netherlands, though the iconoclastic uproar of the *Beeldenstorm* (the destructive 1566 storming of the Catholic images by the Protestants) had extended into the North.

Hoefnagel's overall composition and his imaginative juxtaposition of the various elements resulted in a highly personal, multi-faceted, allegorical portrayal of the dramatic events taking place. The realities of historical time were largely ignored. In spite of the inroads of the Calvinists in the Southern Netherlands by 1570, the symbolic Prot-

xxiv. Detail of the Monogram (Hoefnagel, 1570)

estant image is still of Luther and not of Calvin. Luther sits in a boiling tub in the Mouth of Hell, in much the same manner as do the Christians in a Valenciennes stage setting of 1547 (NR XXV). In fact, the print itself reads like a morality play and parallels theatrical endeavors of the *Rederijkers*, those members of the popular rhetorical-theatrical associations. Numerous dramas, songs, prints, and paintings of the period attest to the close interrelationship of the arts.

In the etching's most amusing element (NR XXVI), a choir in monk's garb, caricaturized in part by animals of the night (an owl, a bat, a frog, and a snake), sings:

> Martini Lutheri fraudes
>   damnarunt Christiani.
> Lupus voravit oves.
> Rex Catholicus regnat vivus.
> Missus DUX ALVA spes nostra,
>   Alleluia.

> Christians are damning the
>   tricks of Martin Luther.
> The wolf has devoured the sheep.
> The lively Catholic King rules.
> The dispatched Duke of Alva is our hope,
>   Alleluia.

xxv. Valenciennes Stage Setting (Anonymous, 1547)

The choir is Bruegelesque. Such prints as Bruegel's 1557 engraving (NR VIII) with its singing donkey may have provided moments of inspiration. The powerful impact of Bruegel's art can be detected in the spirit of the work as well as its graphic details. The print is related in concept and in even greater detail to the *De contemptu mundi* print (CATALOG NR 6) and to another image, *The Throne of the Duke of Alva*, issued anonymously in 1569 (CATALOG NRS 7 and 8). From this latter image and its group of chained women held in tow by the Duke, comes the central focus of Hoefnagel's allegory. Representing the Seventeen Provinces, the enchained form an image which achieved great popularity. The figures appear and variously reappear in numerous prints and paintings.

Among the chained figures only the province of Brabant seems clearly recognizable, and that by virtue of her wealth rather than her coat of arms. Though her shield in *The Throne of the Duke of Alva* bears Brabant's arms, in the *Allegory* it portrays the Greek legend of the Judgement of Paris. Like the figure of God Almighty about to fire a skull-tipped arrow from his crossbow (in the upper right corner), Brabant's shield emphasizes the interpretation of Alva's rule as divine judgement. Hoefnagel appears to have adapted the actual images from an emblem book, such as Barthelemy Aneau's *Imagination poetique* (NR XXVII). Aneau's work, which would have been familiar to Hoefnagel, was published in Lyon in 1552 in both Latin (*Picta poesis*) and French editions.

Alva and the hated Cardinal Granvelle both appear twice in Hoefnagel's print.

Though Granvelle had in fact left The Netherlands six years earlier, he was much on people's minds as rumors of his return were widely circulated toward the end of 1570. Philip's regent, Margaretha of Parma, is pictured with Granvelle and Alva in the Mouth of Hell. Draped with a fishnet, her figure is a reworking of her role as the fisher

of confiscated goods in *The Throne of the Duke of Alva II.*

In contrast to the exalted position of the Decretals, the Bible is tossed on the floor of the Mouth of Hell and all but stepped on by the inquisitor. The Catholic Church is the persecuting agent of Satan, and this is as true of the so-called secular powers of gov-

XXVI. The Bestial Choir (Hoefnagel, 1570)

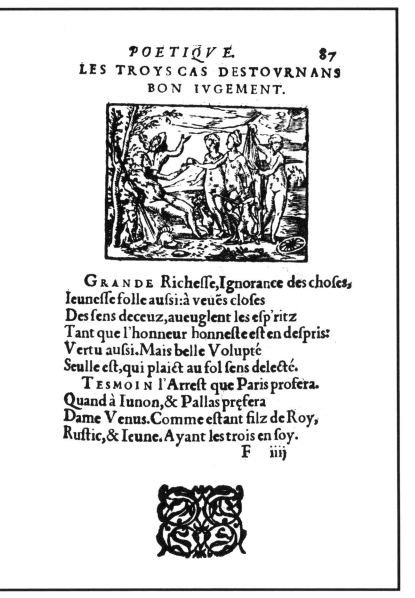

POETIQVE. 87
LES TROYS CAS DESTOVRNANS
BON IVGEMENT.

GRANDE Richesse, Ignorance des choses,
Ieunesse folle aussi: à veües closes
Des sens deceuz, aueuglent les esp'ritz
Tant que l'honneur honneste est en despris:
Vertu aussi. Mais belle Volupté
Seulle est, qui plaict au fol sens delecté.
    TESMOIN l'Arrest que Paris profera.
Quand à Iunon, & Pallas prefera
Dame Venus. Comme estant filz de Roy,
Rustic, & Ieune. Ayant les trois en soy.
                                    F iiij

XXVII. The Judgement of Paris (Anonymous, 1552)

ernment as of the clerical powers. The print, though focusing on the political struggles and emphasizing the enormous civil power assumed by Alva, is aimed as well at the policies and practices of an inquisitorial Church.

Brother Cornelis, the infamous monk whose mock sermons first appeared in print in 1569, is in the pulpit; and Antwerp's newly appointed Bishop Sonnius, a leading inquisitor and an attendee at the Council of Trent, is featured in the midst of chained maidens. Divine Justice, however, is to be meted out by the Almighty who oversees all, from praying Protestants to tyrannous Alva. Hoefnagel's view of divine justice proved to be overly optimistic. The war lasted until near the middle of the next century, and at that, resolution of the religious issues was ambiguous.

Emphases on "rights and privileges" and on "liberties and freedoms" mark many of the early prints and underlie the evolution of Netherlandish democracy. Pamphlets and broadsides were produced in the thousands. Despite the fact that Hoefnagel's political work has been little known, his graphic images are among the most intriguing of the time—the *Patientia* in large part for its subtlety, and the contrasting *Allegory* (etched when Joris had seemingly lost some of his own patience) for its complex attempt to stir the emotions and to strengthen the will of the people in their struggle against the tyranny of Spain.

TWO POSTSCRIPTS:

First: In the summer of 1577, following the Spanish Fury of November 1576 which had ravaged Antwerp and cost the Hoefnagel family much of their wealth, Joris departed from his birthplace yet again. With his friend Ortelius he visited Italy. There he completed numerous drawings, some of which he later used for illustrations in the *Civitates Orbis Terrarum.* When he incorporated his illustration of the Forum Vulcani, the famous Solfatara west of Naples (a drawing now in the National Gallery in Washington), he embellished it with splendid emblematic heads and mallets reminiscent of his *Allegory* (NR XXVIII). Here the "a" of his "last" name is replaced by Georgius, his first name, engraved on a horseshoe nail (a *Hoefnagel*) and set on an anvil rather than etched on a diamond and mounted on a milestone.

Second: Hoefnagel later settled for a time in Bavaria. Beginning in 1581, he worked for several years in Innsbruck for Archduke Ferdinand, creating over a period of nine years a most admired illuminated missal. Also in 1581, back in The Netherlands, the artist Hendrick Goltzius engraved a pair of portraits of Willem of Orange and his wife Charlotte of Bourbon; both portraits are embellished with their sitters' mottos (NRS XXIX and XXX). A set of the prints must have come to Hoefnagel's hands, for, ironically and perhaps with some hint of humor, he included in the decoration for the Archduke's Roman missal the four mottos of Willem and Charlotte, one of several subtle echoes in the missal of life in his beloved Netherlands.

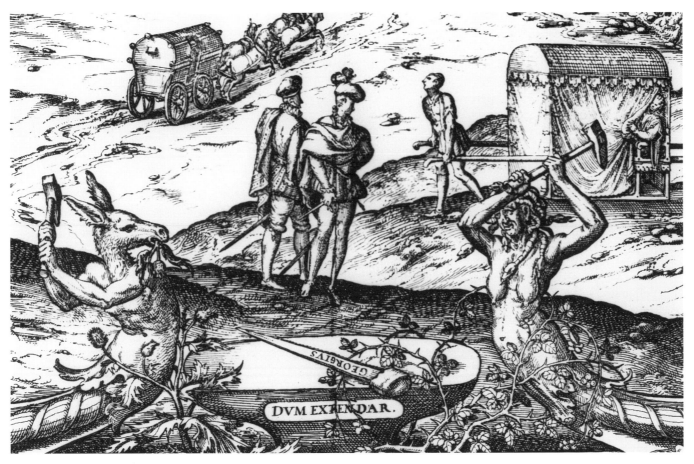

XXVIII. From *Civitates Orbis Terrarum,* part III, nr 58 (Hoefnagel, ca 1580)

23

xxix. Willem of Orange (Hendrick Goltzius, 1581)

xxx. Charlotte of Bourbon (Hendrick Goltzius, 1581)

III

The Duke of Alva & the Prince of Orange

THE BOOM IN PRODUCTION and trade of the printed word and image in the second half of the sixteenth century provided easy access to the tools for propagandists wishing to circulate ideas. Netherlandish production of anti-Catholic or anti-Spanish propaganda under the eyes of the central government in Flanders and Brabant needed to be done anonymously or pseudonymously to avoid prosecution. Prints and pamphlets bearing the names of their makers were only issued in the liberated northern provinces or from safe refuge abroad, most often in Germany or England.

By their nature propagandistic images are produced to glorify and support a position or to defame and oppose one. The simplest means of accomplishing this is by presenting an image in which the "Good" is portrayed as a desirable state or the "Evil" as undesirable. Contrasting these two positions in one image, so that the beholder will

be able to make comparisons, is even more efficient. (See NR IV.) Exaggeration of real or imaginary strengths and the omission of weaknesses, or the reverse, present a still more clear and unambiguous image to the viewer.

The structures described above can be found in many prints with Fernando Alvarez de Toledo, the Duke of Alva and Willem I, Prince of Orange-Nassau, the two main opponents in the first decade of the Eighty Years' War. The earliest prints dealt exclusively with the tyranny of Alva; Willem was introduced as his opponent a few years later, around 1570–1572. Early examples set out to illustrate and make known the tyrannical nature of the rule which Alva had imposed. Several features of this tyranny were established early and returned in almost all of the later works. These included the execution of the Counts of Egmond and Hoorne, Alva's pride, his greed, and his disregard of old privileges.

Probably the earliest image in which the two adversaries, Willem and Alva, were juxtaposed is *Emblematic Contrast of Orange and Alva,* ca. 1570–1572 (NR 16). The composition is clear and effective. Each party occupies its traditionally correct place, in accordance with the description of the Last Judgement in Matthew 25:33: "And he shall set the sheep on his right hand and the goats on the left." The good are placed at God's right hand, i.e., the left side of the print, and the bad on His left hand, i.e., the right side of the image. (Compare NRS 18, 19, and 21 and NR XXXI.) The opponents face each other in the foreground; the background depicts the war which has made Orange and Alva enemies. In this case the scene is the city of Antwerp; several other prints have a globe in the center showing the reasons for the conflict in a more universal context. (See NR 21 and NR XXXI.)

Orange is usually characterized by virtues which govern his life and on which his

XXXI. Vices Rule the World; Truth and Justice Sleep (Theodoor de Bry, ca 1572)

actions are based, and personifications of the benefits which result. Alva in the same sense has vices and their evil consequences as companions. The virtue most commonly associated with Orange is that of Wisdom. Willem is presented as a man whose virtue is directly linked to his religious beliefs, from which follows the grace of God. Resulting from his wise and pious government are, among other personifications, Prosperity, Justice, Harmony, and Peace. Alva on the other hand is led foremost by Envy and Pride. The following list of characteristics might be compiled for the two opponents.

ORANGE	ALVA
Wisdom	Foolishness
Humility	Pride
Benevolence	Selfishness
Honor	Dishonor
Prosperity	Poverty
Truth	Falsehood
Justice	Injustice
Harmony	Discord
Peace	War
Forgiveness	Envy
Love	Hate
Freedom	Captivity
Generosity	Greed
Piety	Blasphemy

In the engraving by Theodoor de Bry from ca 1572 (NR XXXI) Willem and Alva are again contrasted. In the center a globe shows the country terrorized by war and violence. God's right hand reaches down to Willem on the left, who swears to uphold God's commandments. Willem is trying to arouse Justice and Truth who are asleep. On the opposite side Envy, Falsehood, and Lust assault the country, while a figure representing the prosperity of the land is held captive by Alva, armed with a scythe. The punishment which awaits this group is symbolized by the rod of chastisement in God's left hand.

In the first year of his rule Alva established a special tribunal to prosecute and sentence those who had participated in the revolts of 1566 and 1567. This Council of Blood consisted of Spaniards and Flemish yes-men (*Ja-knikkers*, literally meaning "Yes-nodders") among them one named Jacob Hessels who, reportedly, awaking from a doze would merely utter the phrase *Ad patibulum!* ("To the gallows!"). During Alva's reign the Council sentenced an estimated 1100 people to death, and another 9000 had their properties confiscated and were banished. Its most famous victims were Egmond and Hoorne. Even though they had pledged their unconditional loyalty to Philip they were arrested, found guilty, and beheaded. Egmond had been especially popular ever since his cavalry had defeated the French at the battle of St Quentin in 1557.

Contemporary prints and texts often described the course of events. In the final verse of a song from 1568 the writer addresses Alva:

With your teeth dripping with blood
Like Pharaoh and Jezebel,
You come to these Netherlands
As Herod, angry and fierce:
To hang, murder, and burn,
To decapitate all with haste.
So you will be disgraced with Babylon
For all the innocent blood.

The executions soon became a symbol of Alva's cruelty, his thirst for blood, and disregard for the Dutch. The killing of the Counts was often imagined as part of a larger plan, inspired by Cardinal Granvelle to rob the country of its natural leaders so that Catholics could regain absolute control and Alva could rule the country as he pleased.

Another recurring mark of Alva's tyranny was his greed, reflected in the new tax laws, and also the confiscation of the possessions of persons condemned or banished by the Council of Troubles. It was also seen in the raids and looting committed by Alva's soldiers throughout the land. Regarded as the first and foremost injustice was Alva's plan to overhaul tax legislation in The Netherlands. His measures were seen as an attempt to break the legal order and abolish the old privileges. Formerly money had been raised through a decentralized system of levies and tolls in the provinces. The new centralized system, which Alva was ordered by Philip to expedite, consisted of three general measures of which the permanent sales tax of 10 percent on all transactions of moveable goods caused the greatest uproar. This *Tiende Penning* (Tenth Penny) was first installed in 1569 but met with so much resistance that Alva was forced to back down. In 1571 a second attempt to collect the tax met with failure. Although the tax was never really collected, it became a symbol of Alva's greed and proof of his desire to impoverish the citizens of The Netherlands.

The *Tiende Penning* became a favorite subject in anti-Spanish pamphlets and songs. More then twenty songs mentioning the tax are known. Five even carry its name in the title. Notable is the comparison often made between the tax measures and the shearing of sheep. Alva is not satisfied with merely having the wool of the sheep; he also wants to skin and butcher them. (See NR 17.)

In a print deriding Alva's statue in Antwerp (NR 22) the *Tiende Penning* was actually personified by a man in a costume adorned with coins and bearing a standard with official documents and dangling seals. A different print, with a portrait of Orange in the center, presented the tax issue as a battle between a wolf named Alvanus and a sheep

representing Orange, both armed with swords. They stand on opposite sides of a shield bearing ten coins, the tenth coin marked with a cross (NR XXXII).

XXXII. Willem of Orange and the Tenth Penny (Anonymous, ca 1570)

These are rare examples of a straightforward pictorial reference to the tax. Usually the allusions are much less prominent. In several prints, beginning in 1569, a penny bank or a money box is added at the feet of Alva's throne. (See NRs 8 and 13.) They probably refer to the tax but could also simply point to Alva's greed. This hunger for riches can be found in various forms: fishing after confiscated goods (NRs 7, 8, and 13), robbing persons of their possessions (NRs 4 and 11), associating Alva (or the Spaniards) with greed or personifying Greed (NRs 17, 20, and 26).

The cardinal sin of *Superbia* or Pride is another frequently recurring characterization of Alva. Both Christian and Classical tradition condemn aspirations to self-glorification. Allusions to Alva's pride in the pictorial material vary greatly in form, from the use of symbols, such as the peacock or Alva's statue in the citadel of Antwerp, to examples from and references to the Bible. In contrast, Willem is featured as the hero and rescuer of The Netherlands; the goals of his actions are never for his own benefit or glory. They are performed in service of the King and for the betterment of the country and her inhabitants. Often the sacrifices Willem chose to make and the hardships he suffered to achieve these goals are stressed.

It is difficult to pinpoint the precise sources for identifying Alva with pride. General factors such as the Calvinist rejection of outward appearance and ceremony in the Catholic Church, as well as Philip II's dispatch of a foreigner from Spain to straighten out the unruly Dutch, must have played a role from the start. The self-esteem and initial appearance of Alva's well-equipped and trained army would also have made a great impression in The Netherlands. In the print *The Complaint of the German and the Dutchman* (NR 5) the Spanish soldier and Alva are presented as proud and well-dressed, foolishly concerned with their appearances, for their fancy uniforms only superficially conceal their humble origins.

During Alva's tenure as governor his conduct firmly established his reputation as an overly proud man. In many prints in which Alva is featured, he is portrayed sitting on a throne, not unlike a king. (See NRS 7, 8, 11, and 14.) Although this fact is not stressed in the inscriptions, Alva's lofty position is clear, especially when set against the humiliation of the kneeling provinces of The Netherlands. Using his high position Alva terrorizes the land, steals her riches, and kills her inhabitants.

In the spring of 1568 during the earliest organized military operations, the forces of

XXXIII. The Statue of Alva in Antwerp (Philips Galle, 1571)

Willem's brother, Lodewijk of Nassau, were heavily defeated by Alva's troops at Jemgum near Emden in East Friesland. Alva decided that the bronze from the captured canons should be used for casting a statue of himself to be placed in the Citadel in Antwerp (NR XXXIII). The Spanish theologian Benito Arias Montano was responsible for the iconographic program; the statue itself was the work of the Antwerp sculptor Jacob Jongheling. Erected in 1571, the statue portrayed the victorious Alva standing on a pedestal. At his feet was a six-armed two-headed figure representing the defeated forces of heresy and rebellion.

Almost instantly the statue caused an uproar, not only in The Netherlands but also in Spain. It was regarded, especially by Alva's adversaries at the Spanish court, as most inappropriate for a person in the service of the King to glorify himself instead of dedicating his victories to his sovereign. Needless to say, the statue was at least as ill received in The Netherlands. Objections grew from the perception that the statue presented Alva trampling the representatives of the Dutch nobility and states. In addition, approval of the pride and arrogance of a human being announcing his own grandeur and glory was a sin against the Christian principles of humility and self-sacrifice.

The statue was removed from sight in 1574, soon after Alva returned to Spain. It was stored in the citadel until 1576 when it was probably melted down. Its immortality in Dutch propaganda was, however, ensured. In prints prior to 1571, Alva had already been associated with the vice *Superbia*, but after that it was to become a near-standard feature of his characterization.

The statue itself became a symbol of Alva's foolhardy pride and was used as such in later prints. (See NR 27 and NR XXXIV.) The latter depicts the fall of the last three Spanish governors in The Netherlands. While Death has taken, among others, the lives of Luis de Requesens and Don Juan, Alva suffers humiliation. On the left a group of spectators observes the scene and one of them, while kicking Alva, points at the statue in the background as a reminder of the reason for Alva's disgrace. References to Alva's pride were often accompanied by citations from the Bible. The reference here to Job 20:6–7 is typical: "Though he stands high as heaven, and his head touches the clouds, he will be swept utterly away like his own dung, and all that saw him will say, 'Where is he?'" In NR 27 a fool stands beside Alva's throne and points mockingly at a miniature version of the statue. This print contains numerous similar references to scriptural texts dealing with vainglory and pride.

In the *Sendtbrief* of 1573, Willem complained to Philip II about Alva's conduct in The Netherlands. In addition to the matter of the statue, Willem mentioned another example of Alva's haughty conduct. On the occasion of the announcement of the General Pardon in 1571, Willem wrote Philip that "Alva, following the example of the tyrant Herod, took your royal chair, which had never before been touched by any stadtholder, and covered it with a golden cloth, on which he, in your absence, sat like an idol in the crowded square of Antwerp, . . . all this in public contempt and to great damage to your Royal Majesty's honor and reputation." Willem used this anecdote, as well as the issue of the statue, as an example of conduct unworthy of a mere servant of the king.

This strategy was applied in various instances in which Willem contrasted Alva's manner with his own correct behavior, and stressed that he himself had always been most loyal and obedient to the King, and had represented his affairs as well as possible. By doing so Willem justified his actions and the revolt in general, neither of which were aimed at undermining Philip's authority but directed against his disobedient and unworthy servant. Willem thus presented himself as the true defender of the King's honor and territories, and Alva as the cause of all the unrest and problems. This all changed in 1580 when Philip promulgated a ban against Willem. In his response, entitled *Apologie*, published in the following year, Willem strongly attacked Philip as king and as person. A change then became evident in the assessment of Alva's

XXXIV. The Death of Don Juan and the Humiliation of Alva (Anonymous, 1578)

31

reign. Again the servant's (Alva's) cruelty, mismanagement, and pride were described, but now as telltale signs of the master's (Philip's) government.

In many of the prints and in other Calvinist material, a parallel is drawn between the history of the Israelites and the Dutch. Often it focuses on the hardships resulting from God's punishment of Israel by relinquishing her to Assyria (Babylon) after a period of godlessness and wicked kings. Likewise God is perceived to have allowed Spain to establish a tyrannical rule over The Netherlands as a punishment for her sins. Once the people show repentance, God can just as easily end their subjection and liberate them from oppression. In several prints and texts Alva is called the "rod of God," or the "rod of God's anger." (See NRS 7 and 24.) This identification of Alva as an instrument in the hand of God is based on biblical sources, most importantly on the prophet Isaiah, where the Assyrian functions as the instrument which God uses to punish the Israelites. The usage of the biblical term "rod of God" also entails the attribution of pride to the person it describes. In Isaiah the proud Assyrian believes that his power is his own. He is not aware that his power derives from God, or that he has been made mighty only to be used as an instrument in God's hand. When finished, God "will punish the king of Assyria for this fruit of his pride and for his arrogance and vainglory." (Isaiah 10:12.) In later texts it is often Philip who is named the "rod of God," and Alva is reduced to a stick used by the King to beat The Netherlands.

Print NR XXXIV shows the humiliation of Alva after his fall. While on his hands and knees, a personification of Conscience presents him with food and drink in the form of a clump of grass and a trough of blood, in which float the heads of Egmond and Hoorne. This is an elaboration of the humiliation that the Babylonian king, Nebuchadnezzar, suffered, as described in Daniel 4:33: "At that very moment this judgement came upon Nebuchadnezzar. He was banished from the society of men and ate grass like oxen; his body was drenched by the dew of heaven, until his hair grew long like goats' hair and his nails like eagles' talons". In the story of Nebuchadnezzar lies the perfect analogy for any propagandist wishing to draw a comparison with Alva. The story of the mighty ruler who erected a statue of a foreign god and ordered all his subjects to submit themselves and worship the idol or be put to death, offers remarkable parallels to the reign of Alva.

Characterizing a person by comparing or identifying that person with a historical or otherwise well-known character is often done in prints and texts. Both Willem and Alva were regularly presented as contemporary versions of biblical or other later historical figures. In addition to Nebuchadnezzar, infamous biblical and historical figures to which Alva is compared include: Pharaoh, Jezebel, Belshazzar, Antiochus, Herod, Phalaris, Nero, and Attila the Hun. Willem of Orange, on the other hand, is portrayed as a leader of the people, following in the steps of illustrious predecessors like Moses, Solomon, David, Joshua, and Judas Maccabaeus. The 1581 portrait of Willem by Goltzius (NR XXIX) illustrates well the equation made between the qualities of Willem's and Moses' leadership. Three of the four small scenes in the corners of the image show episodes from the Exodus in which God's chosen people are led by Moses from captivity to freedom and which are used as parallels to Willem's leadership. Furthermore, Orange's leadership is to the people of The Netherlands like a guiding bright light in the darkness, just as the pillar of fire which guided the Israelites by night on their journey to the promised land. The fourth image at the bottom right is of a different nature and shows a bird building its nest on rough waters, a personal device and motto symbolizing Willem's leadership as a safe haven during stormy weather. The hand of God drives away the gusting winds so the bird can safely build its nest.

Certain images or stories lend themselves more readily for use as exempla than others. In the story of Saint George slaying the dragon, a well-established exemplum of a courageous victory of good over evil is provided. Both Alva and Orange were used in

xxxv. Willem as St George (Marcus Gheeraerts the Elder, ca 1576)

this same setting by their separate propagandists. The etching by Marcus Gheeraerts the Elder (NR XXXV) portrays Willem as Saint George slaying the dragon and rescuing the princess. As in Hoefnagel's *Allegory*, details of the print are numbered for explanation in a legend. God's Strength, Faith, Truth, and Justice give Willem the strength to defeat the dragon Tyranny, whose parts are identified as Greed, Spanish Inquisition, Hatred, and Killing of Innocents. The maiden saved from the dragon's claws represents The Netherlands, the lamb beside her the Church of Christ.

Contrastingly a small wooden statue shows Alva as Saint George defeating a three-headed monster (NR XXXVI). The three heads are those of some of Alva's earlier adversaries and have been identified as Pope Paul IV, Queen Elizabeth I, and the Saxon elector Johann Friedrich I. This image of a knight slaying a multi-headed dragon can also be related to the story of Hercules defeating the Hydra of Lerna.

Depicting contemporaries in the form of well-known figures is one way of linking the image of one person to established characteristics of another. An alternative means of achieving this same effect is to depict animals acting like humans. Examples of this often originate from animals mentioned in the Bible or in fables. Common in Protestant iconography is the sheep or lamb as a metaphor for the meek and vulnerable Christian who is threatened by Catholic oppression in the form of a predatory animal such as a wolf or fox. These metaphors are less often employed for individuals than for groups of people: nationalities, church members, or professionals. CATALOG NRS 4 and 7 provide good examples of the extensive use of propagandistic animal imagery.

In most countries an animal is used as a national symbol; for The Netherlands this has always been a lion. NR XXXVII shows the Dutch lion fiercely defending the enclosed garden of Holland against an army of Spanish pigs.

At sea the ships of Zeeland, the other liberated province, come to help. They are "manned" by geese. The choice of this bird originates in the Dutch word *geuzen* or *watergeuzen* (beggars or seabeggars), originally a term of abuse, but later a nickname borne in honor by some of the rebels. The image is also a play on *ganzen*, the Dutch word for geese.

The reputation of the Duke of Alva as the bloodthirsty tyrant was so firmly established by Dutch propaganda that he became an instantaneously recognizable symbol for Spanish tyranny and for oppression in general. The phantom of Alva reappeared regularly as a symbol of tyranny in prints, pamphlets, and paintings.

This was true during the years following his return to Spain in 1573, throughout the rule of successive governors, after his death in 1582, and well into the seventeenth century.

XXXVI. Alva Slaying his Adversaries (Anonymous, ca 1560)

34

Cessez Pourceaux de rompre ma Haye,
Retire ta hure, & ton Groin-verrat,
Ou tu recepuras mortelle playe
De ma Massue, ou par mon Geux Soldat:
Mon Excellent Protecteur Orangeat,
Te fera l'assaut, par Mer, & par Terre:
Prens tes Truyes-ladres pour ton debat,
Et fuy-ten Goujerts, fay ailleurs la guerre.

Houdt op in mijn Thuyn te wroeten Spaensche Beeren/
Wilt uwen Verckens-rop tor/ achterwaerts trecken/
Oft mijn Giestige Cudse sal u soo ghebleeren:
Die u thooft sal breken/ oft den hals doth recken:
Den Edelen Prince daer-ghy meed' woudt gherken/
Sal u te Water/ en Land' bespringhen// all:
Vertreckt met u vuyl Soghen/ en Jonghe Spercken/
Loop Suytts loop/ oft Stijn u daer-toe dwinghen// sal.

XXXVII. Stop Rooting in my Garden, Spanish Pigs (Anonymous, ca 1572)

35

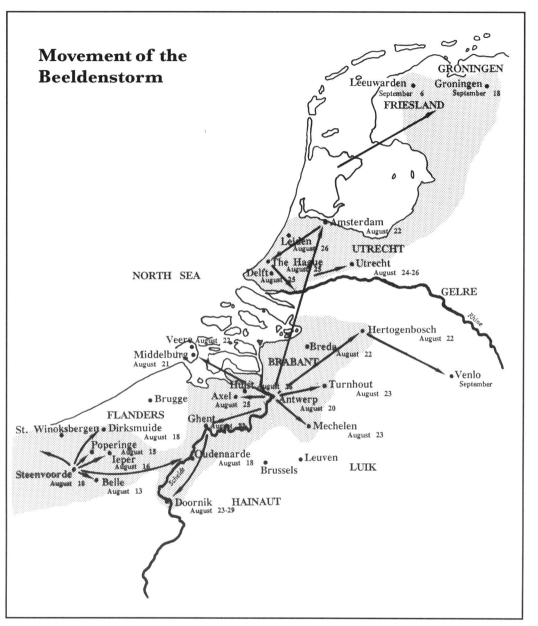

Movement of the Beeldenstorm

GRONINGEN

Leeuwarden
September 6

Groningen
September 18

FRIESLAND

NORTH SEA

Amsterdam
August 22

Leiden
August 26

UTRECHT

The Hague
August

Utrecht
August 24-26

Delft
August 25

GELRE

Rhine

Veere August 22

Hertogenbosch
August 22

Middelburg
August 21

Breda
August 22

BRABANT

Venlo
September

Huist

Turnhout
August 23

Brugge

Axel
August 23

Antwerp
August 20

FLANDERS

St. Winoksbergen
Dirksmuide
August 18

Ghent

Mechelen
August 23

Poperinge
August 13

Leuven

Ieper
August 16

Oudenaarde
August 18

Brussels

LUIK

Steenvoorde
August 10

Belle
August 13

Doornik
August 23-29

HAINAUT

THE BEELDENSTORM
The shaded areas of this map highlight the sections of the land most effected by the storming of the churches. The dates under the names of cities and towns and the direction of the arrows indicate the rapid spread of the *Beeldenstorm* in the summer of 1566.

THE NETHERLANDISH LION LEO BELGICUS II
In 1598 Johan van Doetecum the Younger revised Michael Aitzinger's map, elaborating it with portraits of political leaders. This 1650 printing by Claes Jansz Visscher, labelling the northern and southern sections as "the two Netherlands," is the first such map to refer to the permanent separation resulting from the 1648 Treaty of Münster.

LEO BELGICUS

TIS AL VERLOREN GHEBEDN OFT GHESCHETEN
ICK HEB DE BESTE CANSE GHESTREKEN
1566

LAET ONS WEL BIDDEN SONDER OPHELDEN | LAET ONS RAS KEREN EN WORDEN NIET MOE
OCH DAT ONS HEYLCDOM TE MEER MACH GELDEN | WANT AELE DEES CREMEKIE HOORT DEN DVYEL TOE

1

EMBLEMATIC PRINT OF THE ICONOCLASM

Anonymous
Engraving, 1566
17.8 x 22 cms
Rijksprentenkabinet, Rijksmuseum, Amsterdam

Literature: F.M. 479A, K. en P. 13.
Willem van Oranje: Om vrijheid van geweten, Amsterdam, 1984, nr B 13.
Peter-Klaus Schuster, "Bilderkult und Bildersturm" in *Luther und die Folgen für die Kunst,* Munich, 1983, pages 144–145.

[Vluchtende Duivel]
Tis al verloren ghebeden oft ghescheten
Ick heb de beste canse ghestreken

[Biddende Katholieken]
Laet ons Wel bidden sonder ophelden
och dat ons heylichdom te meer mach gelden

[Protestantse Beeldenstormers]
Laet ons ras keren en worden niet moe,
want aelle dees cremekie hoort den duyvel toe

[Absconding flying Devil]
To pray or to poop, 'tis all in vain.
I have had my best chance.

[Praying Catholics]
Let us pray without ceasing,
In the hope of preserving our sanctuary.

[Protestant Image Breakers]
Let us sweep quickly and not become weary,
For all these paraphernalia belong to the Devil.

The Iconoclasm *(Beeldenstorm)* first erupted in early August 1566 in the poor industrial region of Western Flanders. (See map, page 36.) The origin of the forces which culminated in the outburst can be found in a combination of factors. The economic situation had deteriorated notably in the previous years which, in combination with several severe winters, hit the lower class especially hard. Increased Calvinist preaching, which followed the relaxation of restrictions, placed special emphasis on the condemnation of the widespread use of carved and painted images in the church. This sparked a reaction among small groups of Calvinists who set off to nearby churches to destroy the statues and paintings. In the same month the movement spread rapidly in the South and also to the northern provinces of Holland, Zeeland, and Utrecht. In all, about five hundred churches were attacked. In some of the cities, however, the magistrates succeeded in protecting churches, sometimes by removing works of art from the churches before they could be destroyed.

This print, one of the few contemporary prints showing the iconoclastic fury of 1566, depicts a group of soldiers sweeping up broken statues and liturgical objects which have been removed from a church, as the scene in the background illustrates. Sweeping with brooms (foreground) and scrubbing with a broom and a bucket of water (background) indicate the cleansing nature of the Iconoclasm; the churches once "dirty" with images are now being "purified." The words in the inscription at the bottom right are spoken by the soldiers but are at the same time directed as an appeal to the beholder to continue in the cleansing of the churches. On the left a bishop, a cardinal, and other clergy kneel before an idol portraying a pope, like the Whore of Babylon, riding the Seven-headed Beast. They encourage each other to pray unremittingly that their church may prevail. At the top of the scene the Devil is seen fleeing, clutching in his arms as many objects as he has been able to rescue before they are destroyed by the iconoclasts.

Nach wenigh Predication   Das bildens türmen fiengen an   Kap Monstrantz, kilch, auch die altar   Zerbrochen all in kurtzer stundt
Die Caluinsche Religion   Das nicht ein bildt dauon bleib stan   Vnd weß sonst dort vor handen war   Glich ger vil leuten das ist kundt.

41   Anno Dñj.   M. D. LXVI. XX Augusti

2
THE ICONOCLASM

Frans Hogenberg (before 1540–ca 1590)
Etching, ca 1570
First published by Frans Hogenberg in 1570
20.8 x 28.2 cms
Rijksprentenkabinet, Rijksmuseum, Amsterdam
Literature: F.M. 413/102, K. en P. 8.
P.-K. Schuster, "Bilderkult und Bildersturm," pages 146–147.

Nach wenigh Predication	After a little preaching
Die Calvinsche Religion	Of the Calvinist religion,
Das bildensturmen fiengen an	The breaking of images commenced
Das nicht ein bildt davon bleib stan	Which left no statue standing.
Kap, Monstrantz, kilch, auch die altar	Cowl, monstrance, goblet, also the altar
Und wess sonst dort vor handen war	And all else that was at hand,
Zerbrochen all in kurtzer stundt	All was broken in short time
Gleich gar vil leuten das ist kundt	As many people soon learned.

Hogenberg's illustration of the storming of the images in The Netherlands was probably made some four years after the event. The print was published for the first time in 1570, as the third in a series of twenty prints illustrating the events and first skirmishes which took place in The Netherlands between 1566 and 1570 and which presaged the Eighty Years' War. The prints were etched and published in Cologne, where Hogenberg had fled after being banned by Alva in 1568.

In his foreword Hogenberg states that little need be said, because any knowledgeable person is aware of the origins of the terrible revolt in The Netherlands. He then, nevertheless, recounts briefly the events which preceded the scenes he has illustrated in the prints. The origins of the religious troubles and "war between the Duke of Alva and the Prince of Orange" stem from the measures ordered from Spain by Philip: the harsh edicts and decrees against the "followers of the New Religion," the installing of the new bishops in The Netherlands, and the Spanish Inquisition.

Hogenberg uses a conveniently dissected church to show all the possible forms of destruction of the church decorations. The destruction takes place at night, as is indicated by the various persons bearing torches. Statues are being pulled from their pedestals and chopped to pieces and stained glass windows are being broken. Further back in the church a man with an ax attacks a triptych standing on the altar, while two others tear liturgical garments to pieces. The two guards in the foreground do not seem able to take any action to prevent the iconoclasts from carrying out their business. Both point rather helplessly towards two men leaving the scene bearing torches and clubs, presumably heading towards their next target.

The text under Hogenberg's print refers to the preaching of the Calvinists, shortly after which the destruction started. The print shows also those less driven by religious fervor: two women leaving the scene with their aprons bulging with goods, while on the right two men carry away bags and a large basket. Behind them a man descends the stairs of the sacristy beside the church, hunched under an enormous sack, no doubt also filled with looted goods. Through the windows of the sacristy several of the perpetrators can be seen helping themselves to food and drink, while in the cellar wine gushes from the bashed wine barrels.

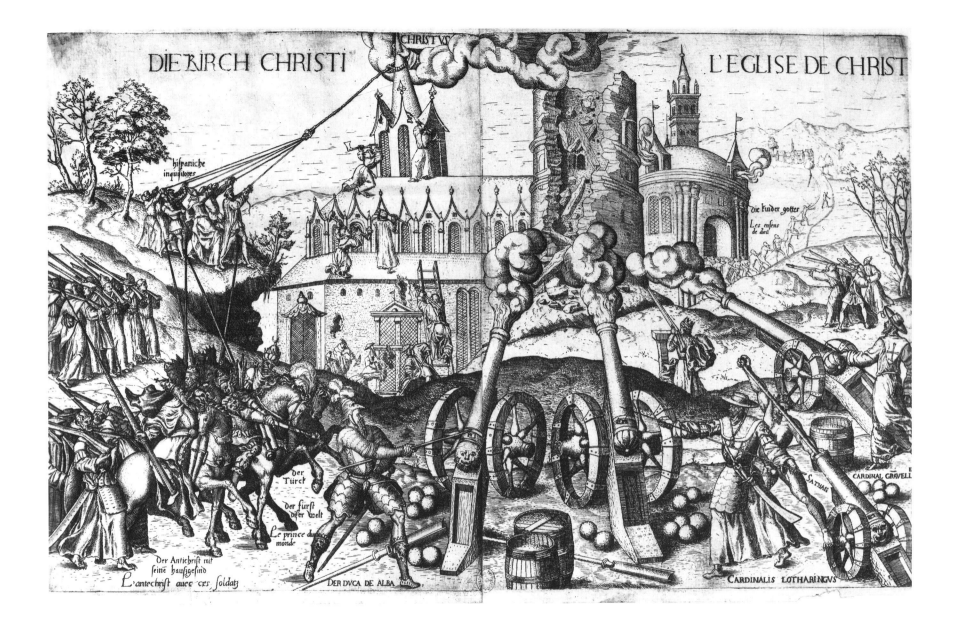

3
THE CHURCH OF CHRIST
(DIE KIRCH CHRISTI / L'EGLISE DE CHRIST)

Anonymous
Engraving, ca 1568
28.6 x 44 cms (printed from two plates)
Bibliothèque Nationale, Cabinet des Estampes, Paris

Literature: See F.M.S. 435A; A.V.S. 342.
Willem van Oranje: Om vrijheid van geweten, nr B 11.
Petra Roettig, *Reformation als Apokalypse*, Bern, 1991, pages 158–159, figure 74.

The image of the destruction of the church is used not only in a more or less historical setting, as in the prints of the iconoclastic fury, but also symbolically as shown here in an anonymous print titled *Die Kirch Christi / L'Eglise de Christ*. The Church of Christ, which is meant to represent the True Church, in this case the Reformed Protestant Church, has come under attack; its worshippers, The Children of God (*die Kinder Gottes*), flee to safety. The nakedness of these believers is an expression of their innocence and vulnerability.

The assault on the church is undertaken by a combination of forces from all sides. Named the Antichrist with his soldiers *(der Antichrist mit seinen haussgesins)*, the ruler of this world (*der furst diser Welt)*, and the Turk *(der Turck)*, the commanders of the attacking forces, the pope, the emperor, and the Turk, direct the siege from the left. They represent the three persecuting forces: the Roman Catholic Church, the world-ly powers, and the infidels. Behind them more reinforcements arrive on the scene.

In the left background a group of the Spanish Inquisition attempts to pull down the steeple of the church, but it is kept in place by the hand of God, reaching down from the heavens. Several monks and members of the clergy armed with axes and hammers have climbed on the church to break up the structure.

With three large cannon in the center and right of the image, the main attack is executed by three of the most infamous persecutors of the Protestants in The Netherlands and France. (Compare NR 13–4.) The left cannon is fired by *Der Duca de Alba*, the center by *Cardinalis Lotharingus* (Cardinal of Lorraine), and the right by Cardinal Granvelle. In the corner, bottom right, Satan prepares a fourth cannon for firing. Several other figures, among them a queen, perhaps Catherine de Medici, also take part in the imaginative attack.

Although the image of the Church of Christ under attack by the forces of evil can be regarded as an established type, its usage in this instance has a specific historic significance. The presence of Alva places the origin of the print in the years 1567–1573 and relates it directly to the events in the Low Countries. The iconoclastic fury of 1566 caused an outrage in the Catholic Church and ultimately led to Philip's sending of Alva. This print can be seen as a Protestant defensive reaction to Catholic indignation at the Calvinist destruction of church decorations. The print maintains that the real destruction of the True Church was not by the Protestants during the Iconoclasm, but was perpetrated by the forces of the Antichrist.

This print seems to have survived in Dutch collections only in an incomplete state. The Rijksprentenkabinet, Atlas Van Stolk, and the Museum Mr Simon van Gijn all possess only the right half of this engraving.

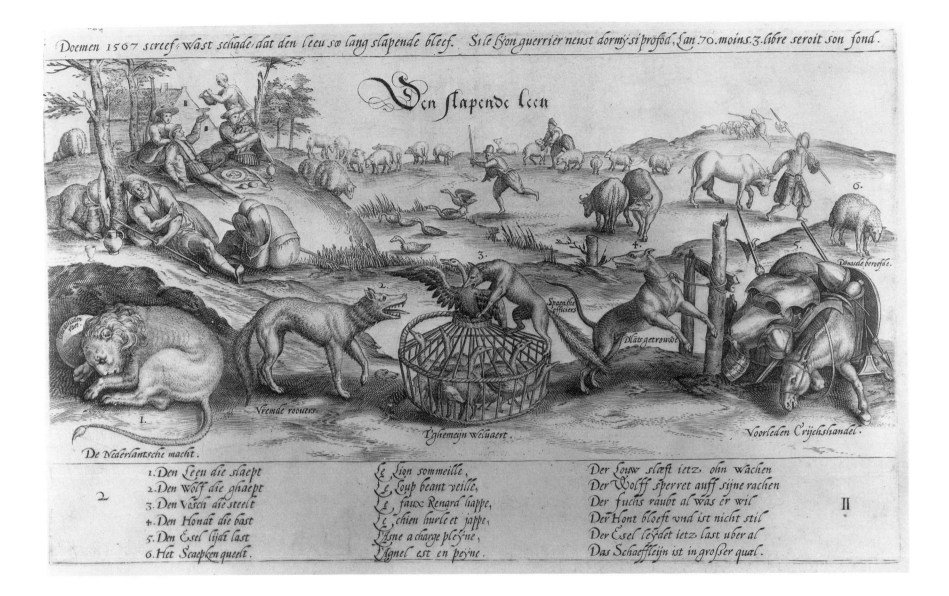

Doemen 1567 screef, wast schade, dat den leeu soo lang slapende bleef.   Si le Lyon guerrier neust dormy si profod, san.70.moins.3.libre seroit son sond.

Den slapende leeu

De Nederlantsche macht.

2	1. Den Leeu die slaept	Le Lion sommeille,	Der Louw slæft ietz ohn wachen
	2. Den Wolf die ghaept	Le Loup beant veille,	Der Wolff sperret auff sijne rachen
	3. Den Vosch die steelt	Le faux Renard liappe,	Der fuchs raubt al was er wil
	4. Den Hondt die bast	Le chien hurle et jappe,	Der Hont bloeft vnd ist nicht stil
	5. Den Esel lijdt last	L'Asne a charge pleyne,	Der Esel leydet ietz last uber al
	6. Het Scaepken queelt.	L'Agnel est en peyne.	Das Schaefflejn ist in grosser qual.

II

4
THE SLEEPING LION
(DEN SLAPENDE LEEU)

Hieronymus Wierix (?) (1553?–1619), after Willem van Haecht I
    (active ca 1552–1577) or Marten van Cleef I (1527–1581)
Engraving, 1579 (?)
19.8 x 31.8 cms
Stichting Atlas Van Stolk, Historisch Museum, Rotterdam

Literature: F.M. 524a; A.V.S. 719 II.
M. Mauquoy-Hendrickx, *Les Estampes des Wierix*, Bruxelles, 1978–1983, nr 1664.
Wolfgang Harms, *Deutsche illustrierte Flugblätter des 16. und 17. Jahrhunderts, Die Sammlung
    der Herzog August Bibliothek in Wolfenbüttel*, Munich, 1980, volume 2, pages 68–69, nr II, 35.

Doemen 1567 screef,	When one wrote 1567,
wast schade dat den leeu soo lang slapende bleef.	'twas a shame that the lion remained asleep so long

1. Den Leeu die slaept	1. The Lion sleeps
2. Den Wolf die ghaept	2. The Wolf gapes
3. Den Vosch die steelt	3. The Fox steals
4. Den Hondt die bast	4. The Dog barks
5. Den Esel lijdt last	5. The Mule suffers
6. Het Scaepken queelt	6. The Lamb bleats

Looking back at the year 1567, this allegorical print bewails the detriment caused The Netherlands by refraining so long from taking action against the Spanish oppression.

The criticism is one of missed chances for intervention, directed primarily at the leaders who for too long allowed their country to be robbed of its riches and its inhabitants to be killed. This message is illustrated on two stages: in the foreground, symbolized by animals; at the back the same message is repeated, acted out by a mixture of animals and personifications.

The Common Wealth of the country *(T'ghemeijn Welvaert)*, represented by the geese and pigs in a basket-like cage, is being robbed by a fox who is identified as Spanish Officers *(Spaensche officiers)* and threatend by a wolf named Foreign Thieves *(Vremde roovers)*. Even though the watchdog Loyal to the Nation *(Dslants getrouwe)* barks alarmingly, his attempts fail to arouse the sleeping Dutch Forces *(De Nederlantsche macht)*, represented by the lion resting its head on the cushion of False Council *(Gheveijsden raet)*. Unheeded and at the mercy of her predators, the lamb, Innocent Deprived *(Donnosele beroofde)*, at the far right, bleats and begs for protection. The mule Former Arms Trade *(Voorleden Crijchshandel)* has broken down under the weight of its load of armor and weapons.

In the background the shepherds who should be guarding their animals have fallen asleep and several other rather distinguished men (most likely representatives of the States General) are shown entertaining themselves with food, drink, and female company, while the Spanish soldiers raid the unattended herds. The shepherd, disappearing with his flock over the hill at the top right of the print, seems to refer to the many citizens who fled from The Netherlands on the arrival of the Spanish forces in 1567, seeking refuge in safer countries like England and Germany.

Hochtutscher lanss   Spaniart   Alba   enus   Hollander ?

Ei lieber wir ert its waren frome lanset vermart
Om gelt zü dinen dien heren getrouwen
Nu leeht onss Duck Alba dem bedelers art
Dass thün dye heiloese Spansche rabauwen

Wir machten sichkoruen ware ongheachte schariante
Vnd fechden ock dass rochüs in Spanien ongheacht
Hir sin wir heren vnd stolte trauanten
Dess willen wy vorstain dass paüpstlich gslecht

Ermails plegen wir die nerong zü hantirem
Lüstich zu wasser vnd zü lant gmachlich
Albanus fiant onss hefft kriahen leeren
Als Christid wir tegen he vechte dasser ich

46

5

THE COMPLAINT OF THE GERMAN AND THE DUTCHMAN

Anonymous
Etching, ca 1567–1569 (handwritten under the print: "1573")
19 x 27 cms
Rijksprentenkabinet, Rijksmuseum, Amsterdam
Literature: F.M.S. 525B.

Hoichtuitscher lanss
Ei lieber wir ertits waren frome lanset vermart
Om gelt zu dinen dien heren getrouwen
Nu leehrt onss Duck Alba dem bedelers art
Dass thun dije heiloese Spansche rabauwen

Spaniart/Albanus
Wir machten fichkorven waren ongheachte schariante
Und fechden ock dass rochus in Spanien ongheacht
Hir sin wir heren und stolte travanten
Dess willen wij vorstain dass Paupstlich geslecht

Hollander
Ermails plegen wir die nerong zu hantirenn
Lustich zu wasser und zu lant gmachlich
Albanus fiant ons hefft krighen leeren
Als Chrislud wir tegen hen vechten dafferlich

High German lansquenet
Alas, once we were brave and renowned lansquenets.
To earn money we faithfully served our masters.
Now, the Duke of Alva teaches us the beggars' art.
All because of these impious Spanish ruffians.

Spaniard/Alva
We wove fig baskets, were unrespected good-for-nothings
And swept chimney-stacks in Spain unesteemed,
But here we are masters and proud fellows,
So we will champion the Pope's cause.

Dutchman
Erewhile we practiced our trades,
Lustily on the seas and just as easily-going on land.
Alva the enemy has taught us to wage war.
Now as warriors we bravely fight against him.

When news of the iconoclastic fury of 1566 reached Philip II, he was deeply shocked and dispatched an army to The Netherlands to restore order. The Duke of Alva, nicknamed the Iron Duke, had strongly advocated a military solution. When in November 1566 the King finally chose a hard-line approach, the Duke was awarded the task and embarked on this mission with an army of some 9500, mostly Spanish soldiers.

When Alva arrived with his forces in Brussels in August 1567, Margaretha of Parma, appointed by Philip in 1559 as regent of The Netherlands, realized that Alva was now in charge and resigned within the month. Before leaving, she dismissed her army which consisted mainly of German mercenaries.

These are the events to which this print refers. The German soldier on the left complains that, since Alva and his Spanish armies arrived, he is no longer employed and has become a beggar. Indeed, his uniform is ripped and worn and his lance lies discarded at his feet. The Spanish soldier has experienced the reverse. Once a simple chimney sweep, he is now a proud officer and gentleman. He no longer needs the broom and rope, attributes of his former profession. The reference to weaving baskets for figs points to one of the less vicious names of abuse the Dutch had for the Spaniards, *vijgemandenvlechter*s (weavers of fig baskets).

The effects on the Dutchman have also been far-reaching. He has abandoned his former peaceful professions as merchant and fisherman to take up arms against Alva and the Spaniards. As an expression of his commitment to his new profession, he raises his shield against Alva who, standing under a small canopy, gazes defiantly out of the print at the beholder.

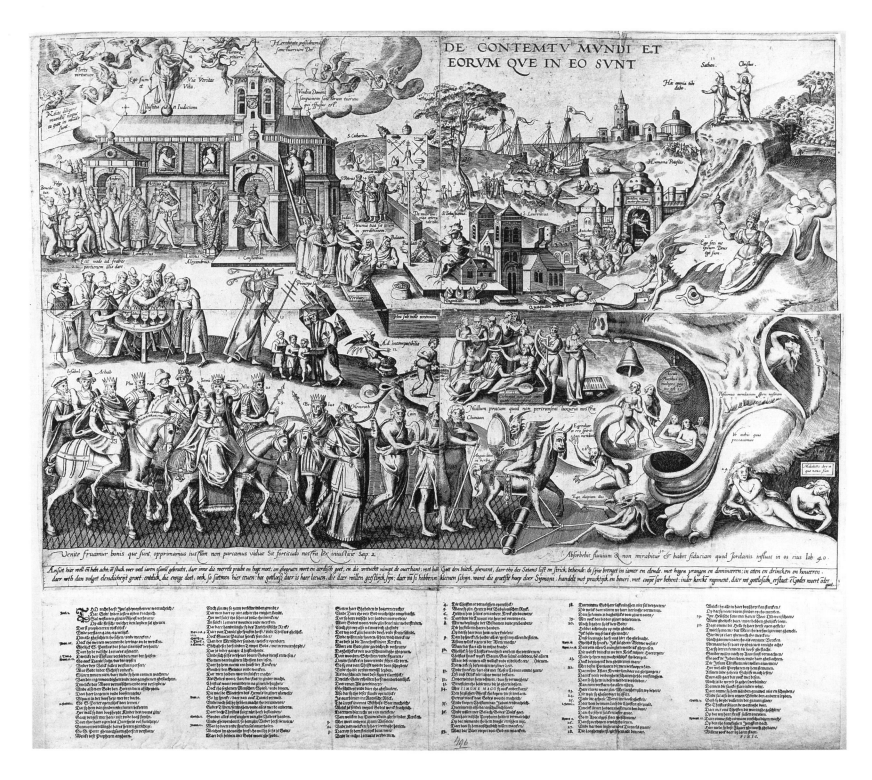

6
CONCERNING CONTEMPT OF THE WORLD (DE CONTEMPTU MUNDI)

Anonymous, after the drawing attributed to the School of van Orley
Engraving, ca 1550–1560
61 x 67.5 cms (plate 47 x 67.5 cms)
Stichting Atlas Van Stolk, Historisch Museum, Rotterdam

Literature: F.M.S. 422.
Karel G. Boon, editor, *The Netherlandish and German Drawings of the XVth and XVIth Centuries of the Frits Lugt Collection*, Paris, 1992, volume 1, pages xxvi–xix.
Christian Tümpel, "Die Reformation und die Kunst der Niederlande" in *Luther und die Folgen für die Kunst*, pages 309–310.

Ansiet hier well ende hebt acht;	Look here carefully and pay attention,
een stuck voer veel iaren tsamen gebracht,	a piece brought together many years ago,
daer inne die werrelt pracht en hoge moet;	in which the world's pomp and pride
an ghegeven wort en aerdisch goet;	and earthly goods are discovered,
en die untucht nimpt de overhant;	and lewdness takes the upper hand,
met han Gott den bueck ghenant,	They name their stomach their god.
daer tho des Satans list en strick behende;	Added to that, Satan's craftiness and clever snares
de sijne brenget in iamer en elende.	bring his own into calamity and misery.
met hogen prangen en domineeren;	With great pressure and domination,
in eeten en drincken en hoveeren.	in eating and drinking and entertaining,
daer wth dan volget elendicheijt groet:	out of which follows great misery,
entelick die ewige doet,	finally eternal death,
oeck so sietmen hier eeuen:	just as one even sees here.
hoe gottloess daer is haer leeven.	How godless there is their life,
die daer willen geestlijk sijn:	those who would be spiritual,
daer van si hebbenn kleenen schijn.	of that they have little pretense.
want die groetste hoep doer Sijmoni:	The greatest hope through Simony,
handelt met pracktijck en bouri.	handled with tricks and thievery,
met coopen seer behent:	with very clever purchasing.
inder kercken regiment,	In the Church's hierarchy
daer wt gottlosick erstaet:	a godless reputation emerges,
en Godes woert onder gaet.	and God's word goes under.

This beguiling print, probably engraved in the late 1550s, relates in an undetermined and equally intriguing way to a very similar and much earlier drawing in the Rijksprentenkabinet. (See Essay I, pages 6–7.) The anonymous artist who first created the image was intent on conveying a sense of the perilous state of the Church, resulting from wicked leaders in both church and state. The image itself would seem to be one of the earliest surviving graphic expressions of the religious reform movement in The Netherlands. The lengthy poem printed separately and appended to the print elaborates on the content of the engraving and its text, transcribed here. As noted in Essay I, it also discusses (all too enigmatically) the origin of the work.

In addition to demonic drolleries, Satan is seated in the center, saying, "Just give me your souls and I will give you the world's power." As the words echo the biblical account of Jesus's temptation, the print recalls the event in a vignette in the upper right hand corner.

The porcine Mouth of Hell clearly had the greatest impact on the overall scheme of Hoefnagel's *Allegory*, though other design touches are recalled in his etching. The complexity of the engraving's program and the numbering of the print's elements, while not unique to *De contemptu mundi*, were also mirrored in the elaborate detail of Hoefnagel's design. (Though the "p" of *contemptu* is present in the drawing's text, it was dropped by the print's engraver.) Aside from the print's obvious influence on Hoefnagel's *Allegory*, its ideas may earlier have influenced the anonymous *The Church of Christ* (NR 3).

7
THE THRONE OF THE DUKE OF ALVA I
(DER STUL DER DUC DE ALBA I)

Anonymous
Engraving, 1569
22.5 x 28.5 cms
Stichting Atlas Van Stolk, Historisch Museum, Rotterdam

Literature: F.M. 518, A.V.S. 409, K. en P. 58.
R. P. Zijp, "Allegorie op de tirannie van Alva," in *Geloof en satire,
anno 1600*, Rijksmuseum Het Catharijneconvent, Utrecht, 1981.

Hie kan man warhafftig sehen, zur ewigen gedechtnusz, alle
Execution und verfolgung die der Duc de Alba gethan hat under
die Evangelisten im Nederland, von Anno 1567 bis auff dise zeit.
Gott der Allmechtig wolle alle ding zum besten wenden.

Here one can truly see, for an eternal remembrance, all executions
and persecutions which the Duke of Alva has done among the
Evangelicals in The Netherlands, from the year 1567 until this time.
God the Almighty will turn all things to the best.

The great popularity of this anonymous print is evidenced by its enormous impact on future anti-Alva prints and paintings. It is reproduced in several prints with only minor changes (for example NRS 8 and 12); the Hoefnagel print (NR 10) reworked its major elements into a broader presentation; and numerous painters continued to create variations well into the seventeenth century.

In place of a traditional imprint in the lower right corner, the engraver has added: "Printed outside the city. In the year 1569." *(Gedruckt buiten Civilien. Anno 1569.)* Based on the strong German element in the dialect of the print's text, one might consider "outside of Cologne," for example, more likely than "outside of Antwerp or Brussels."

In the lower left Cardinal Granvelle, also called "the sly fox," bellows in the ear of the Duke of Alva that the Duke should further persecute and martyr the Evangelicals. To the left of Granvelle and Alva, the Devil presents them with the papal tiara and the crown of Spain, as rewards to both for their endeavors. Above Alva's head is written in Latin, German, and French "the rod of God," pointing to the belief of many that God was using Alva to punish the people for their sins. The provinces, represented by seventeen chained maidens, are held in slavery, while the members of the States General stand silently by, fixed on stone pedestals. Though the 1566 petition of the nobles for toleration *(Verbond der Edelen)* had at first appeared to have improved the situation (NR XXXIX),

its longer-term effect on Philip was precisely the opposite. The lack of follow-up by the States was bemoaned here, as well as in *The Sleeping Lion* (NR 4).

In the background the torture and execution of the Evangelicals goes forward. Egmond and Hoorne are beheaded, their blood creating a lake from which a cardinal fishes out a money pouch, representative of their confiscated property. Instruments of the Inquisition decorate the baldachin over Alva's throne. The ancient rights and privileges have been torn up and thrown on the ground.

Like most effective cartoons before and since, the engraving gains its appeal and effectiveness from its exaggeration and oversimplification of the truth.

52

8

THE THRONE OF THE DUKE OF ALVA II

Anonymous, after the above anonymous engraving
Engraving, 1569 (?)
28.5 x 40 cms
Rijksmuseum Het Catharijneconvent, Utrecht
Literature: F.M. 515.

This simplified version of the previous print makes a few interesting changes. The anonymous artist adds a typical round pottery penny bank in the foreground, indicative of Alva's greed and the imposition of the "Tenth Penny" tax. The artist also changes the fisher of confiscated goods from a cardinal to Margaretha of Parma, a change which persists in later versions. (See NR 12.) The engraver omits the numerous descriptive identifications which the original print had added in both Germanic and French dialects, but appends a long narrative French text.

The artist also added the names "Vergas" and "Del Rio" to two of the supporters on Alva's left. Jan de Vargas was a Spanish lawyer who accompanied Alva to The Netherlands and who had the greatest influence in the Council of Blood. Lodewijk Del Rio, half Spanish and half Netherlandish, was also a member of the Council.

The names "Backerzele" and "Stralen" mark the two men being decapitated on the platform next to Egmond and Hoorne. Antoon van Straelen was a wealthy banker, a close friend of Willem of Orange, and a politically powerful mayor *(burgemeester)* of the city of Antwerp, Jehan de Casembroot, Heer van Backerzeele, was a learned Latin poet and writer, who served Egmond as secretary and counselor. He was repeatedly tortured and interrogated, but remained faithful to Egmond and to his Catholic faith to the end.

Backerzeele had been one of some two hundred presenters of the petition of the nobles (NR XXXIX). Though it was generated by Protestants, the petition was signed by many Catholics as well. Called in the English of the day "The Compromise of the Nobles," the petition was an attempt to persuade Philip's regent, Margaretha of Parma, to replace the religious persecution of the Protestants with a policy of religious toleration. It was on the occasion of the presentation that the petitioners were first dubbed "the Beggars."

xxxix. Frans Hogenberg, *The Presentation of the Petition of the Nobles*, ca 1570; part of the same series as print NR 2.

54

9
PATIENCE
(PATIENTIA)

Joris Hoefnagel (1542–1600)
Manuscript emblem book, 1569
42 x 28.5 cms
Bibliothèque Municipale, Rouen

Literature: Facsimile, edited by Rob. van Roosbroeck, published by "De Sikkel" in Antwerp, 1935.
Karel G. Boon, "*Patientia* dans les gravures de la Reforme aux Pays-Bas," in *Revue de l'art*, volume 56, 1982, pages 7–24.

	Patiente Enamorado			The Patient Lover
El enamorado:	Jo le beso las manos, madama hermosa:		The Lover:	I kiss your hand, lovely lady.
	Gendigate dios, cara de Rosa			God bless you, rosy-faced one.
	De vous servier mon coraçon desire.			My heart longs to serve you.
La querida:	Señor spaeniaert, señor don calf van Lire,		The Beloved:	Señor Spaniard, Señor Don Alva of Liria,
	Gaet mij van hire, want ick en ghelooft nijet,			Go from me here, for I do not believe you.
	Ghij sult nijet op doen, en breckt toch			You will bring all to nought,
	u hooft nijet			And not worry your head about it.
El negritto:	O que dolor es al dolorido:		The Negro:	O how painful it is for the smitten one
	Amar, querer, y no ser querido.			To love and not be loved.

Among the twenty-four emblems created for this album by the Antwerp artist Joris Hoefnagel, only this one bears unambiguous reference to the Duke of Alva.

The phrase *señor don calf van Lire* plays on the word *calf* (the same word in Flemish and English) and an elision of the name *Duc Alfa*.

As described in Essay II, many of the drawings depict the Netherlanders' plight under Spanish domination. Here "The Netherlands," portrayed as a Flemish maid, resists the advances of the Duke while his servant looks on, providing the commentary. Each emblem focuses on patience under stress or trial, as does Pieter Bruegel's *Patientia* (NR XIV). Bruegel shows the ravages of war in the upper left, yet its quotation, which is derived from *Institutiones V* of Lactantius, stresses the importance of patience for the righteous, who live under unrighteous rulers.

While briefly residing in England, Hoefnagel created this emblem book for Johannes Radermacher, a wealthy Flemish merchant and art collector. Radermacher also served as an elder in the Dutch Church in London, a center for refugees from the troubles in the Low Countries.

10
AN ALLEGORY OF THE SPANISH TYRANNY

Joris Hoefnagel (attributed to)
Etching, 1570
41 x 96 cms
Bryn Mawr College Library

SONNIVS VALLE

10
AN ALLEGORY OF THE SPANISH TYRANNY

Joris Hoefnagel (1542–1600) (attributed to)
Etching, 1570
41 x 96 cms
Bryn Mawr College Library, Bryn Mawr, Pennsylvania

Consciously drawing on two popular prints for theme and design, Joris Hoefnagel gave his imagination free reign as he further embellished his creation with story elements from many other sources. Essay II explores some of these relationships, but it is impossible to determine how many details in this imaginative pasticcio came directly from other prints or drawings and how many simply reflect images then in common currency. The world which produced the emblem book was one in which each beast or bird took on meaning. Though the use of images to depict ideas antedated the evolution of the alphabet, the emblem book as a specific genre was a Renaissance product .

Many figures are numbered, but several numbers have been rubbed off in part or in full. With the use of infrared, a magnifying glass, and some logical conjecturing, it has been possible to relocate most of the original eighty-five numbers. Unfortunately, no key exists to explain them. Perhaps the print was designed to have an appendage at the bottom, like the *De contemptu mundi* print, or a separate descriptive pamphlet as did a few prints of the era. There is no trace of an attachment to the bottom, and

the only other cited copy of the print (last seen and noted by François Brulliot in 1833) also lacked a key. There is no known contemporary reference to the print, so one is left to the work's own content to determine its place in the events of the day and its meaning in the mind of the artist.

Did Hoefnagel devise as engaging verses for this print as he had for his *Patientia* emblem book? The names of many of the figures can be established—sometimes by historical personages and other times by traditional emblematic or allegorical figures. Some identifications are debated and some riddles remain. For example: Does the sword-wielding figure with three canine heads, poised to decapitate Egmond and Hoorne (lower central panel), represent Cerberus, the three-headed dog who guards the entrance to Hades, or the three heads of the Council of Blood: Vargas, Del Rio, and the *Jaknikker* Hessels? Or is the former image, perhaps, an allusion to the latter?

Each of the chained figures represents one of the seventeen provinces. In the foreground is Brabant, wealthiest of all the provinces and dressed accordingly. Her elaborate garb is re-

vealing of Hoefnagel's great interest in contemporary costume. As seat of Antwerp, Brabant was also Hoefnagel's home province. She carries in her hand not only the shield depicting the Judgement of Paris (discussed in Essay II, page 21) but also the flaming sword of judgement, mirroring the sword carried by the avenging angel above.

Unlike the similarities of appearance among the young women comprising the provinces in other prints (NRS 7, 8, 12, 17, 27, and 28), differences of many kinds distinguish the figures in Hoefnagel's etching. He may have had very specific identifications in mind for each of the other chained figures, though the missing key has left them to conjecture.

Above the dated milestone in the lower right section of the central panel are three figures: a chained cleric protecting a woman from the advances of a bearded cloven-hoofed man. Although all of the other chained figures in the print are women, here the chained figure is a man in clerical garb. The woman may represent the region of Utrecht; the cleric is possibly Willem Veuzels, Dean of St Peter's in Utrecht; and the interloper is King Philip, as pictured in print NR 13–1. Horned Alva, decked out with instruments of torture, stands to the left behind them. On Philip's order Alva had levied taxes on all provinces; Utrecht refused to pay, claiming exemption on its ecclesiastical status. Alva denied the claim and further revoked Utrecht's traditional privileges. The clergy reacted by sending Veuzels to Spain to seek protection for the province. History records that he "acquitted himself splendidly and with boldness." The tax was, in fact, never collected, and Alva's successor later restored the privileges.

In the lower right hand corner of the print various notables are brought together, bearing out art historian A. E. Popham's observation that Hoefnagel was possessed of "an irrepressible passion for anecdote." Bishop Sonnius, just appointed to his office in Antwerp in 1570, promulgates the teachings of the Council of Trent. He uses a millstone marked *Inquisition* for a lectern, which rests on the back of one of the provinces. Granvelle, with another province under his bestial feet, tears apart a cloth with the hands of "Faith and Hope" and of "Unity"; with his right hand he falsifies an earlier agreement he had made with Philip of Hesse after the latter's defeat in a battle in Germany. The story was told that during the night following the signing of the treaty, Granvelle was said to have altered *einiges* to *ewiges*, turning Philip's punishment "without *any* imprisonment" to read "without *perpetual* imprisonment." Though the incident had been almost a quarter of a century in the past, it was still widely heralded in The Netherlands of 1570 as evidence of Granvelle's scheming and duplicitous nature. Today's historians still debate the details of the event.

As Alva dominated happenings in The Netherlands, so his actions dominate the content of the print. Perched two-faced on his throne, like the Prince of Hell, he is supported and surrounded by accomplices both historical and emblematical. He has removed his gloves, re-vealing his armored hands. Above the group Charles, Cardinal of Lothringen (Lorraine), flies with bat wings and a serpent's body, emblematic of his evil, though brilliant, ways. He is bearing papal gifts to Alva, symbols of the Pope's encouragement of the Duke's defense of the Catholic Church. (See also NR 13–2.) To shade Alva, the figure of Envy, with her head full of snakes, holds a parasol of peacock feathers, signifying false pride.

Behind Alva is Granvelle; at his right hand may be Lodewijk Del Rio. With his animal feet, the right hand figure could also be Karel, Count of Berlaymont, who was referred to as one of Granvelle's "little foxes." It was Berlaymont who first termed the petitioning nobles *Geuzen* (Beggars). The small half-canine figure by Alva's throne may be Viglius van Aytta, with Berlaymont labeled one of Granvelle's "little foxes." Aytta, from within his Catholic post, actually tried to mitigate the plight of the Protestants, and was, therefore, judged somewhat unjustly by the Netherlanders, while at the same time being held suspect by Alva.

Other details of this complex composition add to the image of discord portrayed by Hoefnagel. Again his unrestrained imagination, revealed in this long-lost-and-forgotten print, reemerges to engage the viewer, challenge the chronicler, and inform the art historian.

Perhaps Hoefnagel's press and personages are reflected in this 1627 print (NR XL) from Adriaan Valerius's *Neder-lantsche Gedenk-clanck* (Netherlandish Tune of Remembrance), a book of songs written to recall the events of the freedom struggle. The numbered figures are:

1. The Pope
2. King of Spain
3. Alexander Farnese
4. Duke of Alva
5. Don Fadrique, Alva's son
6. Cardinal Granvelle
7. Vargas
8. Del Rio
9. Bishop of Yperen
10. Brother Cornelis
11. The Press of Suppression
12. Netherlandish Lion *(Leo Belgicus)*
13. Broken Lion's Crown
14. Broken Freedom
15. Torn Privileges of the Land

XL. *The Plight of the Netherlandish Lion*, 1627.

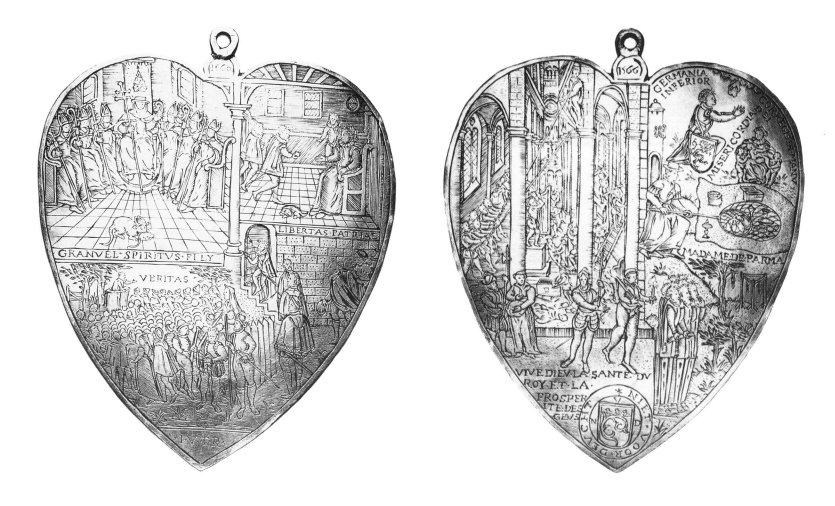

11
PENDENT ON THE TROUBLES IN THE NETHERLANDS

Anonymous
Engraved silver medallion, after 1570
6.8 x 7.7 cms
Rijksmuseum Het Koninklijk Penningkabinet, Leiden

Literature: K. en P. 55.

This anonymous silver medallion recalls the events of the 1560s. In the upper left Cardinal Granvelle, with his six newly appointed bishops, sits enthroned; nearby a cat wearing a cardinal's hat plays with a captured mouse, symbolic of Cardinal Granvelle's role vis-à-vis The Netherlands. In the upper right Margaretha of Parma receives the petition of the nobles to soften the anti-Protestant edicts. Beneath her is written "Freedom of the Fatherland" *(Libertas Patriae)*. In the lower section one sees the Protestant outdoor preaching, the so-called hedge-preaching.

On the reverse of the heart-shaped medal Frans Hogenberg's print, *The Iconoclasm* (NR 2), is reproduced on the left and elements of *The Throne of the Duke of Alva* (NRS 7 and 8) are on the right. The purpose of the medallion is not known, nor is the date of its creation, although the engraver's sources were available by late 1570.

MARGARETHA OF PARMA
Portrait by Karel van Sichem, fl. 1600–1624, after a portrait by his father, Christoffel van Sichem I, 1546–1624.
Engraving from Emanuel van Meteren's *Niederländische Historien* Antwerp, 1611.

J. P. Vinnius exc. Middelburgi 1622.   Cum privilegio confoed. Belg. Provinc. in Septennium.

A. Hertoch van Alba. H. Egmont en Hoorn.
B. Card. Granvelle. I. Heer van Batenburch.
C. Ian Vergas. K. Heer van Backerseele.
D. Loys del rio. L. De Provintien.
E. Bisschop van Yperen. M. Prevelegien gescheurt.
F. Broer Cornelis. N. De Staeten.
G. M. de Parma vist int bloet. O. Goedts Woortsonder wet.

62

12

THE THRONE OF THE DUKE OF ALVA III

Willem Jacobszoon Delff (1580–1638), after a drawing attributed to Adriaen Pietersz van de Venne (1589–1662)
Published by Jan Pietersz van de Venne of Middelburgh
Engraving, 1622
42 x 57 cms
Stichting Atlas Van Stolk, Historisch Museum, Rotterdam
Literature: F.M. 514, A.V.S. 408–II, Hollstein V, nr 97a.

Afbeeldinghe van den ellendighen staet der Nederlanden, onder de wreede tijrannije van den Hertoghe van Alba.

A picture of the miserable state of The Netherlands, under the cruel tyranny of the Duke of Alva.

Between 1609 and 1621 the Twelve Years' Truce in the Eighty Years' War was in effect. Elements of a permanent peace plan were at first resented and then later detested by overlapping religious and political groups, the Calvinists and the Orangeists. They sought a reunion of the Northern and Southern Netherlands. To arouse anti-Spanish and anti-Catholic sentiment to resume the war, these groups revived the old emotionally charged imagery of the 1560s and 1570s. Very popular among these depictions was *The Throne of the Duke of Alva,* developed in numerous painted versions and in this handsomely engraved print. The reproduction on the back cover of this book is of a rare hand-colored copy. Both copies are from the collection of Atlas Van Stolk.

The artist has combined elements of both of the earlier versions and vastly embellished the setting. Background events in the earlier prints became wall hangings in the new one. One looks in vain, however, for any weighty evidence that the artist had seen or used Joris Hoefnagel's variation on the theme.

Letters "A" through "O" mark the major figures. They are helpfully identified in the key below, providing identifications which clarify elements of the earlier prints as well:

A. Hertoch van Alba
B. Card. Granvelle.
C. Ian Vergas.
D. Loys del rio.
E. Bisschop van Yperen.
F. Broer Cornelis.
G. M: de Parma vist int bloet.
H. Egmont en Hoorn.
I. Heeren van Batenburch.
K. Heer van Backerseele.
L. De Provintien.
M. Prevelegien gescheurt.
N. De Staeten.
O. Goodts Woort, onder voet.

In van de Venne's print the two men about to be beheaded, in addition to Egmond and Hoorne (H), are the brothers Gijsbert and Diderik van Batenburg (I), leaders in the movement for toleration and among those who had signed the petition of the nobles in 1566. They are presumably the two unnamed men about to be executed "at Brussels" in *The Throne of the Duke of Alva I.* (Backerzeele and Straelen, depicted on *The Throne of the Duke of Alva II,* were executed at the ancient prison of Vilvoorde outside of Brussels.) Van de Venne places Backerzeele (K), with his hands tied, on the platform to Alva's left.

Second to Alva's left is Maarten Rythovius, Bishop of Yperen (E), who, though unnamed in engravings NRS 7 and 8, appears to Alva's left in the earlier prints as well. It was Rythovius who was priest to Egmond at the time of his execution. Together with several other clerics, he later tried in vain to advise Alva to moderate his tax policies. He does not appear among those included in Hoefnagel's print, possibly because of his seemingly more moderate stance at that time.

13

ALVA'S MISSION TO THE NETHERLANDS AND THE EFFECTS OF HIS TYRANNY
(A series of four prints)

Anonymous
Engraving, 1572
Each ca 18.5 x 13.5 cms
Stichting Atlas Van Stolk, Historisch Museum, Rotterdam
Literature: F.M. 521a–d; A.V.S. 412, K. en P. 59.

1

Coninck philips van spaengien doer synen raet
Vanden bischop ende inquisiturs heeft dat ganse
Neder lant laten comen in groot verdriet

Twee moncken togen nae hispaengien
Eede hebben geclaecht dat sy wt
Haren kercken werden veriaecht

2

Den paus heeft duck dalba dat sweert gedaen
Granvelle ende die herthogin van parma weeten
O wee nederlant isser nu nyet wel aen

Met gelt ende goet doet hem den paus onder
Stant dat die papen moehten houden
Doverhant ock met gewelt en met brant

1

King Philip of Spain, following the advice
Of the bishop and the inquisitor,
Has brought great sorrow to all the Netherlands.

Two monks journeyed to Spain
And complained that they
Were chased from their churches.

2

The Pope has presented Alva with the sword.
Granvelle and the Duchess of Parma participate.
Oh woe Netherlands, now in a critical situation.

With money and goods the Pope supports him
So that the Papists would maintain
The upper hand with force and fire.

This series of rather crude prints is dated 1572, the peak of Alva's reign of terror. Two different sets of the series are known: the one described here, with both Dutch and French inscriptions, is a slightly later copy of the un-dated original which has inscriptions in German and French. The first two prints in the series center on the objectives of Alva's mission, the last two show the results of the consequent tyranny. King Philip receives two monks from the Netherlands who complain that they have been chased from their churches. This is illustrated in a small background scene which shows priests fleeing from their church where iconoclasts, aroused by Calvinist field preaching, are

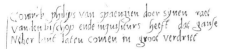

Coninck philips van spaengien doer synen raet
vanden bischop ende inquisitors heeft dat ganse
Neder lant laten comen in groot verdriet

Le roy philip de speue par la playnte des
Eseeks et inquisiteurs a delayssées le pais
bas en grand doleurs 1572

inquisiteur

Rex   Hispani   Eseck

Twee moncken togen nae hispaengien
En de hebben geclaecht dat sij uit
Haren kercken werden veriaecht

Deus moyne se partoyent en espaenie et
Playnderent au roy a grand tristesse
Comme fusitif de leur eglise et abaie   1.

Le pape a donne glayne au duck cruelle
Se soyent a grannelle et parma bien leur cas
Pour ruines ceuls du pais bas

Den pans heeft duck dalba dat sweert
Grannelle ende die hertogin van parma
O wee nederlant isser nu uyet wel aen

parma   Grannelle   alba   pius V papa

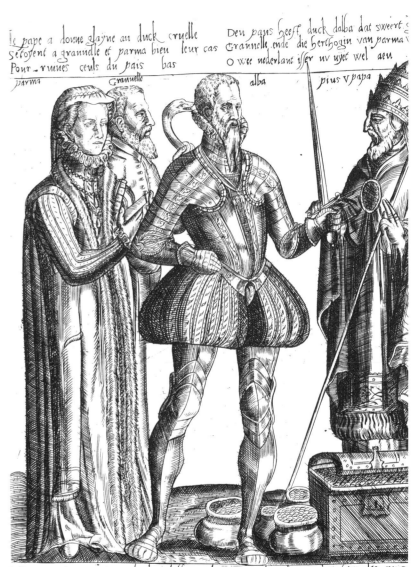

Par or et argent a duck dalba le
Pape fait secours que le prestre
Demorant en leur tours aussi par tiranie

Met gelt ende goet doet hem den pans
Stant dat die papen moehten houd
Douerhant ock met gewelt en met

pulling down and destroying statues. Philip is also advised by a bishop and a member of the Spanish Inquisition who plead for suppression of the uprising.

In the second print Alva is presented by Pope Pius V (1566–1572) with the economic and military means to ensure the superiority of the Church. The sword is used here primarily as a symbol of the violent suppression through military force, but refers at the same time to the Pope's gift to the Duke of Alva of a gold sword and a hat, in reward for his services to the Church. The Duchess of Parma and Cardinal Granvelle support Alva and, by holding a snake to his ear, signify their evil motives.

3

Die scepen vervallen die sciplieden connen
nyet behelpen die copman en vercopt geen
Waer babels hoer is vrolick met ducdalba

Den cramer sit armelyck neder by can
Syn ware nyet vercopen doer ducdalbas
ontlyven schatten en roven

4

Hy nempt met gewelt den ryckdom van
Het lant ende heeft veel ontschuldich
Bloet laten hangen ende branden

Hy heeft ock egmont ende horn dat leven
Genomen ende den heelen edeldom onder bracht
Dat wort van borger en boeren beclaecht

3

The ships fall into disrepair and the seamen are helpless.
The merchant can sell no merchandise.
The Whore of Babylon is merry with the Duke of Alva.

The peddler is condemned to poverty.
He cannot sell his goods because of
Alva's beheading, taxation, and stealing.

4

He seizes with force the wealth
Of the country and has caused many
Innocent people to be hanged and burned.

He has also taken the lives of Egmond and Hoorne
And suppressed the whole nobility.
This is lamented by burghers and peasants.

The third engraving shows the collapse of the Dutch economy (represented by an unemployed sailor, a merchant, and a peddler) which according to the inscription is the result of Alva's killing, burning, and stealing. Meanwhile Alva is embrassing the Babylonian Whore who is accompanied by the Seven-headed Beast.

The fourth and final print is the most vicious in the series. Alva's thirst for blood is translated into the image of the Duke devouring a child, signifying the innocence of his victims. Some of the most fanatical anti-Protestant forces are embodied in a three-headed monster, the heads of which are those of three cardinals: Granvelle and the two French brothers of the House of Guise, Charles, second cardinal of Lothringen (Lorraine) (see NR 3) and Louis, first cardinal of Guise.

A devil wearing a monk's cowl and a rosary inspires Alva by using a pair of bellows to fill his head with evil. The bellows form a popular motif which appears repeatedly in prints of Alva. (See NRS 7 and 8.) Alva tramples under his feet torn and discarded charters, symbolizing the broken promises and his disregard for the Dutch charters.

The anonymous artist also adds the decapitated bodies of the counts of Egmond and Hoorne. The purse in Alva's left hand signifies his greed and the goods he has stolen from the Netherlanders. Representatives of the communities of burghers and farmers wring their hands in despair.

Die scepen veruallen die scipheden conden
Nyet behelpen die copman en vercopt geen
Waer babels hoer is vrolick met ducdalba

Par destruction de nauires le naureurs se
Pouent supporter par faulte de marchandise
Selon duck dalba aueck babilo pred so solas

Den cramer sil armelyck neder hy can
Syn Ware nyet vercopen doer ducdalbas
Ontlynen schatten en rouen

Le marchant son pourement abasis
Ne pouoynt gaigne pour vivre pour
Le ranson du duck et se pilleurs

3

Hy neupt met gewelt den ryckdom van
Het laut ende heeft veel ouschuldich
Bloet laten haugen ende branden

Il prend par fortresse le risesse du pais
Et par sinesse a respandu le sang
Inocens par grand triesse

Hy heeft ock egmont ende horn dat leuen
Genomen ende den heelen edeldom onder bracht
Dat wort van borger en boeren beclaecht

Il a mis a mort egmont et horne et
Tout gentils barons occis par insame que
Bourgoys seu plaint et laboureurs

4

14

THE DECLINE OF THE CATHOLIC CLERGY, or THE CAUSES OF THE DUTCH REVOLT AND THE ICONOCLASTIC FURY
(A series of twelve prints)

Dirck Volckertsz Coornhert (1522–1590), after Adriaan de Weert (ca 1510–ca 1590)
Engraving and etching, ca 1572–1576
Published by Hendrik Hondius I (1573–1650) in 1604
Each ca 12.2 x 20.5 cms
Rijksprentenkabinet, Rijksmuseum, Amsterdam

Literature: K. en P. 67, Hollstein IV, nrs 171–182.
The Illustrated Bartsch, volume 55, nrs 071.1–12.
I. M. Veldman, *De Wereld tussen goed en kwaad: Late prenten van Coornhert*, The Hague, 1990, nr 6.1–6.12.

1) Goodfurchticheit dient God en mensch en wint
   haer broot.
   Piety serves God and Man and earns her bread.

Central in the first print is Piety *(Pietas)*. She is the cause for the existing happy state in which good deeds are performed (giving of alms and comforting the sick) and industriousness flourishes.

2) Het doechtlijc leeven baert gonst bi clein en
   groot
   A virtuous life bears fruit for small and great.

The scene here is almost the same as in the first print. The same persons, both high and low, are now rewarded for their virtuous life with gifts of wealth and power by the figure of Favor.

3) Gonste van prins en volck teelt rijcdom en
   machte.
   The favor of prince and public secures wealth
   and power.

Wealth (the purse) and Power (the charter) are personified in the figure *Divitiae Potentiaque*. Riches and Power have created a strong Church which is shown imposing its authority upon the State. The German emperor, recognizable by the emblem with the double-headed eagle, submits himself to the pope by kissing his feet. (See NR 24 and NR IV.) These achievements also enable the construction of the large buildings on the right, symbols of Wealth and Power.

4) Rijcdom brengt int clooster des vleesches
   weilde zachte.

Wealth brings pleasures of the flesh into the
   monastery.

A consequence of the Catholic Church's newly acquired wealth is disregard of moral standards, leading to the introduction of Carnal Desires *(Delitiae carnis)* into the monastery. The Pleasures of the Flesh are personified by Venus and Cupid (sex) who embrace a rather stout Bacchus (alcohol). The scenes in the background show members of the clergy in pursuit of worldly pleasures.

5) Weelde haer grootmoeder Goodsvurchticheit
   vermoort
   Lust strangles her grandmother Piety.

In the fifth scene Piety, who was featured in the first print, is strangled by her grandchil-

Ipsam delitiæ perimunt luxusque parentem, 5
Weelde haer grootmoeder Goodsvruchtigheyt vermoórt:

Vipereis pietas occubat ipsa modis.
La Volupte estrangle Piete leur grand mere:

En speciem simulans virtutis Hypocrisis astat, 6
In doechts plaets comt schijn-doecht (verchievde vuylheit) voort:

Et cunctos falsis ludit imaginibus.
Hypocise occupe la saincts place.

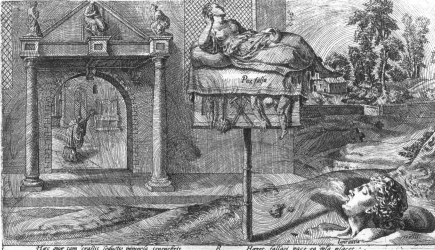

Bellua multorum capitum seducta suum mox 7
Scijn-doecht brengt Verleiding daer tvolc na luistert

Insequitur ducem, hunc fictio Vana parit.
Amenane seduction pleine de audace.

Hæc quæ tam crassis seductio immersa tenenebris 8
Die maect valsche vree in blintheit verduistert:

Hæret, fallaci pace ea ipsa placet.
Laquelle aueugle par paix faux en fallace.

dren, Pleasures of the Flesh. On the left the body of Piety is laid in her grave, while on the right the Pleasures of the Flesh—Bacchus, Venus, and Cupid—are carried triumphantly toward the Church.

6) In doechts plaets comt scijn doecht (verchierde vuijlheit) voort.
   Hypocrisy takes the place of Piety.

All signs of a once pious past have now disappeared. Central in the image is the figure Hypocrisy *(Hipocrisis)* who wears the garments and rosary of a nun and holds a precious standing dish filled with excrement. As the inscription notes, foulness is presented as a precious object. The monkey on her shoulder refers to vice and foolishness. On the right a wolf in sheep's clothing helps a figure into a priest's garb, which nevertheless fails to conceal his hoofed feet. On the left a scholar is forced to eat an object representing a house.

7) Scijn doecht brengt Verleiding daer t'volc na luistert.
   Hypocrisy bears Temptation which the people follow.

Seduction *(Seductio)* is represented as a woman with glasses. A rope on which masks and more spectacles are strung runs from her tongue to a three-headed personification, The People *(Vulgus)*. Following her, they are led toward an abyss. The background shows the people involved in various objectionable, superficial prac-

tices of the Catholic Church: processions, the worshipping of images, and kneeling in front of a small Lady's chapel.

8) Die maect valsche vree in blintheit verduistert.
   Ignorance conceals False Security.

The eighth print presents an image clouded with the emanations of Ignorance *(Ignorantia)*. The resulting darkness brings a blindness which obscures all abuse and gives a sense of false security. Although the personification False Securitry *(Pax falsa)* lies asleep on an altar adorned with liturgical objects and votive gifts, the precariousness of her situation is clear in the unstable support on which she rests.

9) Luther des menschen vuyl en mesbruick ontdect.
   Luther reveals man's falsehood and misuse.

Finally *Deceit Abusus* in the Catholic Church is revealed. The proof is given by Martin Luther who lifts up the cloak of the pope and by the light of his torch, Testimony of Scripture *(Testimonium Scripturae)*, reveals his true nature. The three-headed personification of The People stands in amazement at this discovery. In the background a wolf, dressed as a priest, is exposed to the people by Erasmus of Rotterdam. A simple peasant reading from the Bible, while leaning on his spade, illustrates true Christian religious practice, made possible by the teachings of Luther and Erasmus.

10) Misbruic met dinquisition tot moort verwect.
    Misuse and Inquisition lead to murder.

Not only the Church, but also the worldly power is corrupted with deceit. The ruler from the first print in the series sits on his throne between his two counsellors Abuse *(Abusus)* and Spanish Inquisition *(Inquisitio Hispanica)*. Abuse's true nature is only partially concealed under his cloak and mask. Spanish Inquisition bears instruments of torture (compare NR 15) and a press in which the heart of Christ is crushed.

11) Vervolging doodt Christum in sijn arme scapen.
    Persecution kills Christ through his flock.

Following the advice of Abuse and Inquisition the worldly powers persecute and kill the followers of Christ, the true believers. With a lance Persecution *(Persecutio)* kills both an innocent child and its mother. The nimbus of the child indicates that in murdering the innocent, Christ himself is killed. The background is filled with more scenes of executions.

12) T'oproericht volck veriaecht monicken en papen.
    The rebellious people expel the monks and papists.

The persecution and abuse of power have turned the people to rebellion. Iconoclastic fury follows the chasing of the Catholic clergy from their churches. Revolt *(Seditio)* is portrayed as a figure with two different, male and female, upper parts of the body. They symbolize the self-destruction of a divided community locked in an internal battle.

M. Luterus   *Vulgus*

Et fraudes Cleri et mendacia tecta tenebris   9   Admota primus face Luthere aperis
Luther des menschen vuyl en mesbruick ontdect   Luther du Clergé les grands abus. descoeure

Abusus   *Inquisitio Hispanica*

Hinc et abusus, et hin monet inquisitio cædem;   10   Queis aures pronæ principis esse solent
Misbruic met inqsisition tot moorc verwect   Abus nous met Inquisition en oure.

Persecutio

Hæc quæ persequitur mitem cum corpore Christum   11   Innocuos varijs conficit modis.
Veruolging doode Christum in syn arme scapen   Itelle occist la brebis et son maistre

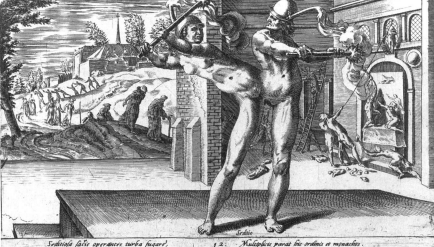

Seditio

Seditiosa faces operantes turba fugaré,   12   Multiplicis parat hic ordinis et monachos.
Top rich volck veiaecht monicken en papen   Dont le mutin enchasse moine et prestre.

72

In this series of twelve prints, engraved after drawings by the Lutheran artist Adriaan de Weert, Coornhert expresses his view of the course of events which led to the deterioration of the Catholic Church and the consequent Iconoclasm and Dutch Revolt. The situation evolves from an ideal state, through the emergence of abuse and hypocrisy, to the state of conflict and turmoil. Only a few historical persons figure in this story; most are personifications. Unlike the propaganda issued by one of the warring parties to propagate its own cause, these prints look back in time and try to give a personal historical and political explanation of the past events.

Coornhert refused to choose sides in the religious conflict in The Netherlands. Although this print series seems anti-Catholic, it denounces only the hypocrisy and abuses which he believed had become incorporated in Catholic religious practice, not in the Church itself. He was no propagator of the Calvinist religion as an alternative to Catholicism. During the 1570s Coornhert expressed his strong disapproval of Calvinist intolerance and various acts of violence committed against Catholics, standing firm for religious freedom and tolerance. These principles brought him into conflict with both sides: first with the central government in Brussels and then with the Calvinists. In 1568 a trial under Alva had resulted in Coornhert's conviction, the seizure of his possessions by Alva's Council of Troubles, and Coornhert's consequent flight to Germany.

Because of his strong condemnation of the Iconoclasm of 1566, Coornhert had been distrusted by the Calvinists. He condemned a Calvinist inquisition as strongly as the Spanish Inquisition. In 1572, after a threat against his life by the hot-headed Lumey, the leader of the Sea-Beggars (*Watergeuzen)*, he was again forced to flee. In 1576 he was finally permitted to return to Haarlem. Coornhert acted as advisor for Willem during those years and both seemed to have held similar views on issues. Coornhert was outspoken, but Willem's position led him to a more diplomatic and reserved stance. Especially in thoughts on religious tolerance Willem and Coornhert held common ground, though Willem realized that a divided country could never stand up effectively against the enemy.

15
THE PERSECUTION OF THE TRUE FAITH

Hendrick Goltzius (1558–1617)
Engraving, ca 1578
Published by Hendrik Hondius I in 1604
24.6 x 18.5 cms
Rijksprentenkabinet, Rijksmuseum, Amsterdam

Literature: A.V.S. 357, K. en P. 34.
The Illustrated Bartsch, volume 3, nr 76–II.
W. Harms, *Deutsche illustrierte Flugblätter*, volume 2, pages 130–131, nr II–71.

An allegory on the persecution of the True Church by the Inquisition, this print cleverly makes use of the two familiar biblical stories of the Judgement of King Solomon and of Christ before Pilate. They are freely interwoven to serve as a vehicle for the print's message.

The King Cruel Ruler *(Crudelis princeps)* on his throne faces two women who represent True Church and False Church. The ruler is blindfolded, not like Justice for impartiality but as a sign of his blindness towards the truth. Instead of seeing with his own eyes, he governs and judges based on the advice of his four gruesome counsellors Doctor Noose *(Doct. laqueus)*, Doctor Sword *(Doct. gladius)*, Doctor Water *(Doct. aqua)* and Doctor Fire *(Doct. ignis)*. The choice he must make here is between the pleas of the mothers, False Church *(Falsa Ecclesia)* and True Church *(Vera Ecclesia)*, each claiming to be the mother of the child Church of Christ *(Christus in membris suis)*. True Church in modest dress kneels, humbly begging for mercy. False Church in her indecent and fancy garments adorned with jewelery grins and makes a mocking gesture in her success at fooling the blind king. The ruler, like Pilate, has decided to have the child, who represents the living Church of Christ, killed by his executioner; the dead child, Barrabas, symbolizes the absence of the spirit of Christ in the False Church. The (unsymbolized) persecution of the Church of Christ is illustrated by the small scenes in the background where Christians, recognizable by the nimbus-like rays of light around their heads, are hanged, beheaded, drowned, and burned at the stake.

The four counsellors don the attire of doctors of theology, but bearing the instruments of torture and execution they represent the methods of the Inquisition—doctors of a theology upheld by means of torture and killing. Although the Spanish Inquisition was never actually installed in The Netherlands, its name was so infamous that it was often perceived as the driving force behind the Spanish policy there.

It is tempting to look for the portrayal of Philip II in the person of King Solomon, and although the features and the youthfulness of the figure do not support a direct attribution, the contemporary beholder must surely have been aware of the similarities between Philip's reign and the government of Cruel Ruler. The notion that the king himself is innocent and cannot be blamed for the violent acts perpetrated by his subordinates on their own behalf, or on advice from the "court," was often expressed in the first decennia of the Dutch revolt. This argument was used to justify a revolt which was not directed against their rightful king but against his servants.

The appearance of the executioner is reminiscent of personifications of Violence or Tyranny (see various figures in NRS 10 and 17) but is likewise not similar enough to make an unquestionable identification with Alva, who really can be regarded as Philip's executioner in The Netherlands, a similarity which could not have gone unnoticed.

On the whole the scene can be interpreted as an image of manipulable government, with a violent executive power, ruled from behind the scenes by forces which encourage persecution and cruelty. Note the owl perched on the throne behind the ruler. As an attribute of Minerva and, therefore, a symbol of Wisdom, the owl would be well suited for the image of Solomon's Judgement. In this print, however, the presence of the owl is more meaningful in its second, less positive form as a night creature, blind in the light of day, a symbol of ignorance or blindness to the truth. (Compare the owl in Hoefnagel's allegorical print, NR 10.) If after all this the beholder still remained in doubt, another clue to the nature of Cruel Ruler's government is visible in the image on the rug lying at the feet of the throne. It presents one of the most wide-spread anti-Catholic images from the Reformation, a wolf attacking a sheep.

The Latin references to Scripture at the bottom of the print refer to the persecution of God's chosen people and warnings against unwise government.

John 16:2   "The time is coming when anyone who kills you will suppose that he is performing a religious duty."

Proverbs 14:28   "Many subjects make a famous king; with none to rule, a prince is ruined."

Proverbs 29:12   "If a prince listens to falsehood, all his servants will be wicked."

Exodus 1:10   "We must take precautions to see that they do not increase any further."

Exodus 1:16   " 'When you are attending the Hebrew women in childbirth,' he told them, 'watch as the child is delivered and if it is a boy, kill him; if it is a girl, let her live.' "

Honor.

Fallac

Inuidia.

PRVD CONS

DIVITIÆ.

BELGICA.

Al Hceft Suc d'alba nedertant naet ghescoren,
En de gemeynte ghebracht in armen staet,
Wat heeft hy nu van sijn fame verloren,
Hoe wel valschs hem croont met den ouden haet,
Maer de Prince door Gods ghenade vrdo in sijn dact,
Vdoleuft Rijdom, en den Lauwerier met Eare,
Dies sijn goede fame ouer al de werelt gaet,
Salich is hy die vetteliyck strijt, voor Godt den Heere.

Duc d'Albe aiant tondu le bas pays, et mis
Le peuple a pourete, ou est sa gloire bonne?
Il l'a du tout perdue, et maints amis exquis,
Iacoit que faulse Enuie en ce gloire luy donne.
Mais le Prince, discret, humble, et bonne personne,
Par le Duin secret, obtient en chascun lieu
Bon-Los, Richesse, et puis, de Laurier la Couronne:
Heureux est qui combat pour la gloire de Dieu.

N.G.

16

EMBLEMATIC CONTRAST OF ORANGE AND ALVA

Anonymous (Theodoor de Bry? 1528–1598)
Engraving, ca 1570–1572
25.6 x 33.1 cms
Rijksprentenkabinet, Rijksmuseum, Amsterdam

Literature: F.M. 525.
W. Harms, *Deutsche illustrierte Flugblätter*, volume 2, pages 46–47, nr II–24.

Al heeft Duc d'alba nederlant naect gheschoren,	Although the Duke of Alva has shaved The Netherlands bare
En de ghemeynte ghebracht in armen staet,	And brought the people to a sorry state,
Wat heeft hy nu dan syn fame verloren,	See how he now has lost his fame,
Hoewel valscheid hem croont met den ouden haet,	Even though Falsehood crowns him with the old hate;
Maer de Prince deur Gods ghenade vroom in syn daet,	But the Prince, in God's grace, pious in his actions
Verwerft Rycdom, en den Lauwerier met Eere,	Earns Riches, and Laurels with Honor.
Dies syn goede fame over al de werelt gaet,	That is why his good fame travels over all the world.
Salich is hy, die wettelyck stryt, voor Godt den heere.	Glorious is he who righteously fights for God the Lord.
Schorst op u lendenen, en vreest druck noch smerte,	Gird your loins, and fear neither oppression nor pain,
Op dat ghe t'paeschlam nut met een oprecht herte	So that you may partake of the Passover lamb with a sincere heart.
Dan sal Godt u vyanden voor u verstooren,	Then God will destroy all your enemies,
Jae als Pharao met hun macht versmooren	Indeed, and as with Pharaoh, crush their power.

The print pictures Willem of Orange and the Duke of Alva standing opposite each other in a landscape with a view of the city of Antwerp in the distance. Both are accompanied by several allegorical figures who serve as characterizations of their rule in The Netherlands. (A reverse copy of this print, with only Dutch names and texts, is also known.)

The date of 1572 would seem the most fitting for the print. This was the year when the revolt against the Spanish took an encouraging turn for the Dutch. The taxation measures Alva had imposed on trade, combined with several failures of the harvest, had brought severe hardship and unrest to many towns. After the capture of the town of Den Briel by the Sea-Beggars on April first, one town after another, though often by force or under threat of the Sea-Beggars, declared their support of the cause of the Prince of Orange. Taking advantage of the change in the tide, he launched a new invasion from the south and east. Our print can be seen as part of Orange's propaganda campaign to raise support for his cause and to bring unrest to the parts of the country still under Spanish control.

Alva on the right holds a pair of shears which he has used to shear the naked and chained personification of The Netherlands of her riches. (Both names *Belgica*, the old Latin name, and

Nederland are used simultaneously in reference to the Low Countries.) The result of his rule is further reflected in the poor condition of The People *(Plebs)*, who are dressed in rags and reduced to begging. Alva's companion, the double-faced Falsehood *(Fallacia)*, carries a torch and a bucket of water as symbols of her deceptive and contradictory nature. Envy *(Invidia)* gnaws on a human heart while the snakes on her head reflect her poisonous scheming.

Willem of Orange, in contrast, is surrounded by virtuous personifications. Wealth *(Divitiae)*, signifying the prosperity of the country resulting from his beneficial government under the grace of God, contrasts with the poverty on the side of Alva. Wise Counsel *(Prud. Cons.)* symbolizes the legality and deliberation on which his government is based. For this the Prince is crowned with a laurel wreath by Honor, and his virtue is made known throughout the world. At the same time Fame heralds the infamous reputation of Alva. The verse under the print stresses the God-given pious nature of Willem's campaign.

The two small scenes in the lower corners illustrate and em-

phasize this underlying religious aspect of the message. On the left side the Israelites celebrate the Passover feast in remembrance of their deliverance from Egypt. The accompanying text is an encouragement to endure and not to fear oppression or sorrow, for then, as the right-hand scene of destruction of Pharaoh's armies illustrates, God will destroy your enemies as he has Pharaoh.

A parallel is drawn between the fortunes of the Israelites and the Dutch, who saw themselves as the chosen people of God. Their oppression under Spanish rule was seen as similar to the situation of the Israelites in Egypt. This concept also further elaborates on the roles of Orange and Alva. Orange, like Moses, will, with the help of God, liberate his people from the tyranny of the Spanish Pharaoh Alva. The story of the destruction of the armies of Pharaoh was frequently used by other artists as an illustration of God's punishment of tyrants. See NR XLI by Hendrick Goltzius.

XLI. Hendrick Goltzius, *The Punishment of Evil*, 1578?

17
THE PLAGUE OF ALVA'S TYRANNY IN THE LOW COUNTRIES

Anonymous
Etching, ca 1573
24 x 31.5 cms
Rijksprentenkabinet, Rijksmuseum, Amsterdam
Literature: F.M.-RPK 518A.

Inn diese figur findestu Guthertziger leser gants
Lieblich abgemalet und ein jeder fur augen gestellet die plage von
Niderlant welche fur anderr nation mit Reichtum und nerung hoich
Erheben Jetzund aber durch die albanische tirannye underr
Welchen sie elendiglich gefangenn und auch grawsam mishandlet
Ligen beraubet geschend und zu nicht getan wirten

Zwo medlin wol getan mit erbarn seden
Darzu von hertsen woll gemut
Des albanisch gross Wuten sint affgetreten
Zum princen sich gebent mit sput

Die edle magt von hollant ein strytbar heldin
Die zeuosche von Walchern mit ihr gants frey
Sitsendt gerust habend forcht onderr ihr fussen hin
Eintracht vertreibt ihr moutereij

Die magt von mechlen dar zu ihr swester von sutphen
Aufs forcht und zweijtracht sint geswecht
Wie das frantsen kunings Veratherreij fur hin
Onehrt die magt henngaw gants frech

Sihe da ligen sie geschent. Verblind al zsamenn
Ghezogen under dalbanische fuss
Suffzen umb hulff zum princen ersamenn
Solchs thut verhindren das phaffs gebruss

In this image you, kind-hearted reader, will find drawn
Quite lifelike and clear to all, the plague of The Netherlands.
Once risen above other countries through wealth and trade,
But now under the tyranny of Alva
They are miserably imprisoned and also terribly maltreated,
Robbed, violated, and brought to ruin.

Two maidens of honorable ways
And with cheerful hearts,
Have hastily made their way
From the anger of Alva to the side of the Prince.

The noble maiden of Holland, a militant heroine,
The Zeelander of Walcheren, truly free as well,
Sit confidently, with Fear under their feet.
Unity drives Mutiny away.

The maiden of Mechelen and her sister of Zutphen
In fear and discord have succumbed,
Like the French King's earlier betrayal
Shamelessly dishonored the maiden Henegouwen.

See the violated and blinded gathered together,
Brought under Alva's foot,
Together they beg the Prince for help.
Such is prevented by the papist brood.

The composition of this indelicate print combines two of the more popular plans on which several of the other prints are based: Alva with the chained provinces of The Netherlands at his feet and the comparison of Alva and Willem of Orange. In the cartouche at the top the author invites the reader to behold this lifelike picture of the plague of "Alvanian" tyranny *(Albanische tirannye)* which has taken hold of The Netherlands, and issues a warning to other countries which might stand to loose their wealth and trade as well.

No longer are all the provinces under the dominion of Alva. (See NRS 7 and 8.) The liberated provinces Holland and Zeeland are now armed and have chosen the side of Orange. They have overcome Fear *(Furcht),* who lies trampled under their feet. Strengthened by their union, Concord *(Eintraht)* drives away Mutiny.

On the other side, however, the remaining provinces are in a sorry state, bunched together and blindfolded, still enleashed by Alva and his Council. Of the kneeling provinces only Brabant, Flanders, and Henegouwen are identified. The province Gelderland *(Geldria)* occupies a more

conspicious place in the image as she is being driven back naked among the captured by *Zweijtragt* (Discord) and *Tiranneij,* the brutal personification of Tyranny. The two opposing camps of Orange and Alva each fly their own characteristic banners. The Christian symbol of the pelican picking its breast to feed its off-

Den Ysel, bevrosen.

XLII. *The Slaughter of Zutphen,* ca 1620; one of a series of sixteen prints created to further the anti-Spanish movement toward the end of the Twelve Years' Truce. The works were issued anonymously with the title: *Spiegel de Spaansche Tiranny in Nederland* (A mirror of the Spanish Tyranny in The Netherlands.) (See also NR XL and NR 12.)

spring typifies the love and self-sacrifice of the Prince of Orange. It is not surprising to find on Alva's banner the familiar image of a wolf with a sheep in its jaws, the bloodthirsty killing of the innocent. (See NR 16.) The documents with attached seals strung to a pole beside the Duke's throne are a reminder of Alva's hated tax bills.

There are several historical events pictured in the print and mentioned in the text which permit accurate dating. The fourth verse makes note of the French King's betrayal *(des frantsen kunings Verathereij),* which must be a reference to the massacre of the French Huguenots, 24 August 1572, the Massacre of St Bartholomew's Night. The cities of Mechelen in Brabant and Zutphen in Gelderland are mentioned in the text and their provinces featured in the image. After joining the side of Orange in the summer of 1572, both were recaptured and severely punished by the Spanish armies then under the command of Alva's son Don Fadrique. The print was made shortly after the recapture of Zutphen and echoes the cruelty of events which followed (NR XLII), thus dating it shortly after November 1572.

18

THE CAPTAIN OF WISDOM and THE CAPTAIN OF FOLLY
(DE HOOPMAN VAN WEISHEYT en DE HOOPMAN VAN NARHEIT)

Theodoor de Bry (1528–1598)
Engraving, ca 1570–1572
Published by Theodoor de Bry
Diameters 12.1 and 12.4 cms
Bryn Mawr College Library

Literature: A.V.S. 413, Hollstein IV, nrs 178–179.
Willem van Oranje: Om vrijheid van geweten, nr C 20.

These circular prints form an elegant pair, illustrating and contrasting Willem of Orange and the Duke of Alva. Willem is presented as a ruler who is led by the virtue of Wisdom, while conversely Alva is the champion of Folly. The small scenes surrounding the portraits serve to illustrate the nature of their respective governments.

The border around the portrait of Orange contains three examples of wisdom or wise government from different periods in time, and places his rule alongside these famous examples. Directly beneath the portrait of Willem, is the familiar biblical example of the Judgement of King Solomon. At the upper left is the Judgement of Cambyses, derived from ancient Persian history, a recurring example in representations of justice. (The Persian King Cambyses ordered the corrupt judge Sisamnes to be flayed and his skin used for the throne on which his son and successor Otanes would sit.) The third example seems to be less an historical scene than an illustration of the wisdom of religious piety in the common man. A man is seated before a meal on a table, and while saying grace remains undisturbed by the temptations offered by Death and the Devil. *Putti* and ornamental figures fill in the circular border.

The verse confirms Willem's status as a contemporary wise ruler:

De hoopman van weisheyt (Le capitaine prudent)

De Wijsheijt welck gheweest heeft voor alle tijden
Soeckt godsalighe vrede tot slants bevrijden
En hout de Prinschen in enen gherusten staet
Sij bemint de Waerheijt en wilt gheensins lijden
Leughen noch bedroch rechtveerdich is al haer daet
Salich is doverheijt diese behout inden raet.

The Captain of Wisdom

Wisdom which has existed through all times
Seeks godly peace towards the nation's liberation
And keeps the Prince in a peaceful state
She loves the Truth and cannot tolerate
Lying or deceit, Just are all her deeds
Blessed is the government which follows her counsel

83

84

The portrait of Alva in the companion piece is very similar to Theodoor de Bry's other illustrations of the Duke. (Compare especially his features and helmet with NR 16 and NR XXXI.) Alva as the Captain of Folly wears around his neck a medallion in the shape of a fool's head. The scheme for the print is the same as that for Willem. The ornamental border consists of three main scenes, each emphasized by a small canopy. Here, however, biblical or historical sources are absent. The three main scenes, together with the intermediate figures of monkeys and fools, form an almost medieval grotesque parade, a compilation of humorous and bizarre drolleries. The verse around the outer border adds a more serious tone to the print. It warns:

De hoopman van narheit (Le capitaine des follie)

Als eenen Tiran den ner, laet wt kycken,
Soo brengt den Tijt zyn vuijlicheid aenden dach,
Hooverdij maect hem sot die wysheid doet
  wijcken,
Sijn eere is schandelijck soot hier blycken mach,
Die goede tot ontsach, die bosse hem beminnen,
Verblintheid der herten maect rasende sinnen.

The Captain of Folly

When a tyrant is a fool, beware,
Time will reveal the mess he makes.
Pride drives insane he who pushes wisdom aside.
His honor is scandalous, as is apparent here.
The good are inspired with fear, but the wicked
  love him.
Blindness of the heart makes terrible madness.

The two prints are meant to be seen together, Willem on the left and Alva on the right, so that the two rulers face one another and their contrasts are most striking. A second pair of round prints exists and is usually considered a pendant of the first pair. The first of these has as subject the virtue of Love *(Charitas)*, and could be regarded as the companion print to Willem, the other features the deadly sin of Pride *(Superbia)*, and would match the print of Alva. Although both of the themes correspond well with the two portraits, *Charitas* is dated 1588, much later than the Willem and Alva. *Superbia* is a reworked version of an older plate of a satire on the pope.

The prints are usually regarded as examples of designs for ornamental silver plates. It is difficult to be certain that the prints were really designed for this purpose; no objects actually manufactured after these designs are known. Judging from the number of copies of the prints that have survived, they seem to have been a commercial success. De Bry, who is probably most famous for illustrations of the early voyages to the Americas, made, beside many ornamental prints, several other anti-Spanish and anti-Catholic prints. Not surprisingly, in 1570 he was forced to flee from the Southern Netherlands to Frankfurt. There he set up a flourishing printmaking and publishing business.

86

19
SATIRE ON THE STATUE OF ALVA

Anonymous
Engraving, ca 1571–1572
34.8 x 48 cms
Rijksprentenkabinet, Rijksmuseum, Amsterdam

Literature: F.M. 569A.
Willem van Oranje: Om vrijheid van geweten, nr C 17.

Aensiet o ghy Nederlander Seer Wyt vermaert
Dat metalen beelt ws tiran seer hooch verheven
Al staet hy vrymoedich stout onvervaert
Hy staet gheheel vercout wilt voor hem niet beven

(Alva)
Tot mynder Eeren en hooghen Name
Heb ick int Casteel van Antwerpen doen Rechten
Dit metalen beelt om verbreden myn fame
Ick heb door myn stercke hant myn vianden slechte
Geheel verwonnen door myn Wysheyt en cracht
Ja haer herten sinnen heb ick berooft met macht

(Den tyt)
Wat verheft ghy U arme eerde en as oncrachtich
Teghen uwen schepper met so hooghen moet
Tontschuldich bloet roept Clachtich
Vraeke over U o tiran Verwoet
Aensiet hier uwen tyt voor handen
Als pharao en antiochus moet ghy in schanden

Behold, o Netherlander widely renowned,
This metal statue of your tyrant standing high.
Although he stands frank, daring, and undaunted,
He is completely frozen, so do not tremble for him.

(Alva)
In my honor and lofty name
I have erected in the Castle of Antwerp
This metal statue to spread my fame.
By my firm hand I have destroyed my evil enemies,
Completely triumphed because of my wisdom and strength.
Yes, with force I have stolen their hearts.

(Time)
How you raise your weak flesh and poor bones
Proudly against your creator.
The innocent blood calls out mournfully,
Revenge upon you, o raging tyrant,
Behold, here the time left to you
Like Pharaoh and Antiochus you shall be disgraced.

(Duivel)

Hert en Cloeck myn sone als een vroom helt
Vreest niet tot deser uren
Al syn U vianden veel en onghetelt
Door mynen raet suldyt wel wtuuren
Hout U als nero tiranich en wreet al U leven
Gelt en ryckdom sy u van my ghegheven

(Tienden penninck)

Aensiet o edel ghenadighe heeren
Desen bequamen tyt
Coemt nu om vruecht vermeeren
Int nederlansche cryt
Een yeder coemt nu halen
Syn herte wel ghemoet
Nu cont ghy prys behalen
Teghen den tiran verwoet
Ick tienden peninck boven maten
Heb die herten af ghewent
So coemt toch nu te baten
Als edel prince exelent
Wilt niet langher vertrecken
Ick maeck u de passagie
Wilt u lansknechten verwecken
Met moet ende coraygie

(Prince Van oraingien)

Te water en te lande heb ick met ghewelt my nu begheven
Als een prince gheweldich wt liefden soeckende de welvaert myns heeren landen
Die door ghewelt schattinghe onrecht en tiranie langhe hebben moeten sneven
Door u duck dalba met uwen bloetraet nydich van verstande

So wil ick nu waghen lyf ende leven met myn edel heeren ghehuldich
Om des conincks landen eendrachtich te stellen in ghoede ruste
Helpt hier toe oock u selven ghy ondersaten so ghy te doene syt schuldich
En niet wederspanich staen teghen my die in u welvaert heb luste
Oft so ghy u onwilich met onverstant wilt rebelleren
So wil u ontmoeten ongheluck en groot verseren

(Devil)

Strongly and bravely my son, like a virtuous hero,
Fear not in this hour.
Although your enemies are many and uncountable,
With my advice you will survive.
Remain like Nero tyrannical and cruel all your life.
Money and Wealth you will receive from me.

(Tenth Penny)

Behold, o noble and gracious gentlemen,
This appropiate time.
Come now to increase the joy
In The Netherlands' realm.
Now each comes to retrieve
His heart in good spirits.
Now you can score easily
Against the fierce tyrant.
I, Tenth Penny, beyond measure
Have turned the hearts away,
So come now to benefit
As a noble and excellent prince.
Do not leave us again.
I have made the way clear for you.
Arouse your lansquenets
With bravery and courage.

(Prince of Orange)

With strength I have now embarked on both sea and land.
As a mighty prince sincerely seeking the prosperity of my lord's lands,
Which have long suffered violence, unjust taxation, and tyranny.
It is because of you, Duke of Alva, with your Council of Blood, driven by envy
I will risk my life and limbs, together with my noble and honorable men,
To restore the king's lands in unity and peace.
Help in this, for your own benefit, citizens, as you are obligated,
And do not recalcitrantly oppose me who seeks your well-being,
Or in the event that you are unwilling, and thoughtlessly seek to rebel,
You will meet with disaster and great harm.

This anonymous print was probably engraved in 1571 or soon thereafter. It shows an adapted version of the statue (compare NR XXXIII) in which Alva tramples Justice and Truth, Widows and Orphans. The Duke is admonished by Time, who holds an hourglass and announces Alva's impending disgrace, a fate equal to that of Pharaoh and Antiochus. On the other side, the Devil, crowned with a papal tiara, comforts Alva and promises him support and rich rewards if he, like Emperor Nero, continues his cruel reign. At the bottom the author directs his words to the Dutch beholder, stating that although the statue is impressive, it is cold, lifeless, and should not be feared. The desired result of this appeal is shown. On the left several *Geuzen* (identified by their beggar's bowls) have literally rediscovered their courage. They had lost heart, but now take repossession of their hearts which were stolen and locked away by Alva. These hearts are seen having been released by the figure standing to the right of the opened door to the pedestal, the figure whose dress is decorated with coins and who bears a standard with sealed documents. This figure is named Tenth Penny *(Tienden Penninck)*, the infamous taxation bill, and he says that he is the reason why so many hearts have turned away from Alva. He also invites the Prince of Orange, together with his mounted officers on the right, to return. In the text above Orange and his men, Willem declares his intentions.

Here one encounters the key issue of the print, an appeal to the citizens of The Netherlands for support of Orange's campaign. The Prince declares that he has been and will continue fighting to restore peace and prosperity in King Philip's domains, too long tyrannized by Alva. Orange is taking the position of the honorable prince, still loyal to his master, only opposing one of his servants whose violent rule is the cause of the revolt and is undermining the King's authority. Orange calls upon the citizens to help themselves, to fulfill their duty, and not to oppose him. He also warns that unorganized revolt will only bring trouble.

Orange's first campaign in 1568 failed partly because of a lack of the support which he had expected from the local population. For his second campaign in the summer of 1572 the situation was more promising, and Orange was better prepared. This print can be seen as part of the propaganda war waged to rally support for the Prince before the actual campaign.

20

WILLEM OF ORANGE KNEELS BEFORE CHRIST

Theodoor de Bry (1528–1598)
Engraving, 1572–1584 (ca 1580)
22.1 x 29 cms
Museum Mr Simon van Gijn, Dordrecht
Literature: F.M. 728A, K. en P. 36.

Den Paus, den Coninck, heur ondersaten mede
Bidden Godt almachtich om peijs en vrede.
Mijn heer de Prinche als een goede voorspraeck
Bidt Godt om verlost te sijn van ergernis en wraeck
Want d'misbruijck soo groot is deur onse sonden,
Dat wij gheplaecht worden tot alle stonden.

The Pope, the King, together with their subordinates,
Pray to God Almighty for peace.
My lord the Prince, as a good intercessor,
Prays God for deliverance from offence and revenge
For the abuse is so great because of our sins,
That we are tormented at all times.

In many prints of Theodoor de Bry nearly identical compositions and images of persons frequently appear. In this case he seems to have borrowed the image of the kneeling King Philip II and Pope Gregory XIII from a print by Wierix. (See NR 22.) Although some of the figures have been copied, the meanings of the two prints are diametrically opposed.

In de Bry's print the desire for peace and the sinfulness of the world are the main topics. A globe of the sinful world is filled with three biblical scenes: the Fall and two episodes from the Apocalypse. The Devil stands behind the globe and calls upon those who seek strange gods to honor and serve him. An angel holds the key and the chain with which the Devil is bound to the globe, and is about to cast him into the bottomless pit for a thousand years. (The Revelation 20:1–3)

Willem of Orange has turned his back to the world and prays directly to Christ to grant peace, so the people can worship freely. Christ answers that sin is the cause of all harm, and that all wrongdoers shall be punished. God's trumpet from above announces that if Christ is followed, no plagues will befall the people. Above Willem and Christ are the tables of stone with the first commandment: "Thou shalt have no other gods before me."

Philip and Gregory kneel with their retinue, which includes Alva, Orange's captive son Philips Willem, an unnamed bishop, and another unidentified person. This group also kneels in prayer, but to ask, in addition to peace, for support for the Church of Rome. Although the text clearly states that they direct their prayers to Christ, their place in the composition is more ambiguous, as they appear to kneel before the Devil and sinful world. (There is also a similarity here with the image in the globe of worldly kings worshipping the Seven-headed Beast.) De Bry may have consciously contrived the ambiguity; they are in any case positioned much further away from Christ than Willem of Orange.

Willem of Orange's son, Prince Philips Willem of Orange, Count of Buren, had been kidnapped in 1568 at the age of fourteen on orders of King Philip II. He was taken to Spain where he was raised in the Catholic faith at the Spanish court. The small scene illustrating the release of Daniel from the lion's den is employed here as a metaphor for Philips Willem's condition as a Protestant among the Catholics.

The message this print propagates is that the source of all the misery and troubles caused by the war is the sinfulness of the world. By disregarding worldly pursuits, forsaking all other gods, and honoring only God through his son Jesus Christ, as exemplified by Orange, can one find the only way to salvation and peace.

91

21
WILLEM OF ORANGE AND HIS WIFE CHARLOTTE OF BOURBON

Theodoor de Bry (1528–1598) (attributed to), after Maarten de Vos (1532–1603)
Engraving, ca 1575
Published by Adriaen Huybrechts I (mentioned 1573–1614)
23.6 x 28.1 cms
Rijksprentenkabinet, Rijksmuseum, Amsterdam

Literature: F.M.S. 702A, A.V.S. 576, K. en P. 106.
M. Mauquoy-Hendrickx, *Les Estampes des Wierix*, nr 1670.
Willem van Oranje: Om vrijheid van geweten, nr A 4.

Den Prince.
O ghenadich Godt, ghy verlost den ontschuldighen
Al staender veel vijanden na mijn leven
Die heere bewaert, die ghetrouwe eenvuldighe
Doen ick vermindert wert, heeft hij mij verheven.   Psal.3.1/6

The Prince:
O merciful God, you deliver the innocent
Although many rise up against me.
The Lord upholds the faithful and modest.
When I was down, he lifted me up.   Psalm 3: 1–6

De Princersse.
Och Godt des hemels schepper der creatueren
Verlost ons vander vremde godloose macht
Vrouwen scheijnders die de weesen haer goet ontvueren
Want ghy zijt alleen onsen troost hulp ende cracht.   Judith.9.

The Princess:
O God, heavenly creator of all creatures,
Deliver us from the foreign godless might,
Violators of women who steal from the orphans,
For you alone are our consolation, support, and strength.   Judith 9

De ghemeynte.
O heere ghij sult die leugheneers versteken
Aenden gheveijsden hebdij een mishaghen groot
En den bloetghiereghen want heur tonghe int spreken
Is flatterende maer hun hertte soect ons doot.   Psal.5.

The Community:
O Lord you shall cast out the liars.
You strongly detest the hypocrites
And the bloodthirsty, for in speech their tongues
Are flattering but their hearts seek our death.   Psalm 5

On 12 June 1575 Willem of Orange married Charlotte of Bourbon. It was his third marriage and followed the dissolution of his marriage to Anna of Saxony on grounds of her licentious behavior.

Although the engraver of this print is not mentioned, it seems safe to attribute the work to Theodoor de Bry on grounds of the similarities with some of his other prints. (Compare NR 20 and NR XXXI.) Only the names of the designer Maarten de Vos and the publisher Adriaen Huybrechts appear on the print.

Willem and Charlotte kneel on opposite sides of a small table or altar which bears their prayer books and Orange's coat of arms and motto.

Their prayers are directed to God whose name is represented by the tetragrammaton, the Hebrew characters which spell Jehovah. This device was frequently used by Calvinists to circumvent the problem of depicting God. On either side and in the distance behind Willem and Charlotte are groups which represent the people of The Netherlands. The group behind Orange contains the upper classes, among them some of his officers; those behind Charlotte represent the lower echelons of society, farmers, and burghers. From out of the heavens two hands reach down above these two groups holding objects which together with the texts express the power of God to intervene in man's life. The hand on the left with the crowned heart held upside down symbolizes the ease with which God can turn around, like the winds, the heart of a king. On the right the hand releases an instrument of punishment, the birch rod. The text refers to the book of Jonah and declares: "If you, like the people of Nineveh, avow guilt, then God will take from you the rod of chastisement."

As in the previous print, the message is a religious one, though with political consequences. Like Willem and Charlotte, the people should lay their fate in the hands of God. All the troubles that have befallen The Netherlands and its citizens can be averted through the power of God, if only they acknowledge their weaknesses, sinfulness, and guilt. This reprimand would seem to refer not only to a general concept of sin, but in light of the comparison to the wicked city of Nineveh, also to holding false beliefs or to idolatry. Given the Protestant (if not Calvinist) audience which the print addresses, this can be interpreted as a call to leave behind old ways, which were unpleasing to God, and to embrace the new faith.

22

CHRIST GIVES THE SYMBOLS OF POWER TO PHILIP II AND POPE GREGORY XIII

Hieronymus Wierix (1553?–1619)
Engraving, ca 1580
19.7 x 27.6 cms
Prentenkabinet van de Koninklijke Bibliotheek Albert I, Brussels

Literature: K. en P. 35.
M. Mauquoy-Hendrickx, *Les Estampes des Wierix,* nr 1667.

The print shows Christ standing before a small altar at which Philip II and Pope Gregory XIII kneel. On the altar lie the King's crown and scepter and the papal tiara with the keys of Rome, symbols of the rulers' worldly and ecclesiastical realms of power. Christ gives the two men his blessing and presents them with a globe which bears a sword, cross, olive branch, and crown. These objects symbolize the government of king and pope, which by upholding the authority of the Church can secure peace by means of the sword.

The image is constructed as a confirmation of the authority on which the governments of Philip and the Pope rest. They are appointed and blessed by Christ. To question the wisdom of their government is to doubt Christ. The references to Scripture, born by the angels on both sides and at the bottom of the print, affirm the print's message: "Fear God, honor the king." The text in the cartouche at the bottom right is an appeal to perseverance by the Catholic believer: "As the Lord lives, your life upon it, wherever you may be, in life or in death, I, your servant, will be there." (2 Samuel 15:21)

It is from this print that De Bry has borrowed the figures of Philip II and Pope Gregory XIII for his view of the Christian rulers. (See NR 20.) The print was made before 1580 (Philip's coat of arms does not contain the conquest of Portugal in 1580) and after 1572, the beginning of Pope Gregory XIII's reign.

Der werlt rinck iss voel van den gheist dess Heerenn Sapientia 1 Cap.

O Nederlant slecht oprechte landenuij
Clijck van sinnen nerstich van handen
Beegaefft de rijcke Goot milldelick
Dor sin genad geedyende rickelick

23
THE GLOBE WITH NETHERLANDISH ALLEGORIES
(A series of four prints)

Anonymous
Etchings, ca 1570–1572
Each ca 17.2 x 21.5 cms
The Metropolitan Museum of Art, New York
(The Elisha Whittelsey Collection, 1957)

1) Der werlt rinck iss voel van den gheest dess Heerenn
   (Sapientia 1 Capt.)
   O Nederlant slecht oprechte landen
   Cluck van sinnen nerstich van handen
   Beegaefft de rijcke Goot milldelick
   Dor sin genad geedyende rickelick

2) Si sin rukelos geworden und hebben hoer selven der
   Idelheijt avergegeven (Eph:4)
   Dye weelde werdrietich eyn lastighe dracht
   Missbruckt gads gave in lust und pracht
   Iver sott bowt den torn van Babell
   Men twisst om twoort dat wert ein fabell

3) Dye quade Werlt / Esaus tyt (4 Esdre:6)
   So dwalt men in seedenn dor twist wt geeloof
   Goot gyfft dat rycke lantt tot eyn rooff
   Enn sendt eyn Roede vredt enn hoichmoedich
   Verderfft landt und luid myt Roevers bludich

4) Wee w, Motten sullen w Beedde syn, Wormen u decke
   (Esai:14)
   Noot dringt tot gott; Noot lehrt biddenn schir
   Goot werpt de geslagen Roeid int fwir
   End strafft Assur stolt nha siner daet
   Hi is wys dye dyt werck gads verstaat (Esai:10)

1) The world is full of the spirit of the Lord.
   (Wisdom of Solomon 1:7)
   O Netherlands, simple upright lands,
   Keen minds, industrious hands,
   Endowed by the plentiful God generously.
   Through his grace you prosper.

2) They have become foolhardy and have given themselves over to
   vanity. (Ephesians 4:19)
   Sorrowfully the Wealth, a heavy burden,
   Misuses God's gift in pleasure and splendor.
   Zeal foolishly builds the tower of Babel.
   Man argues over the word that becomes a fable.

3) The evil world / The time of Esau. (2 Esdras 6:9)
   So man errs by religious disputes.
   God gives the rich country over to plunder
   And sends a rod, cruel and proud,
   To ruin country and people with bloodthirsty robbers.

4) Woe to you, maggots will be your bed, and worms your coverlet.
   (Isaiah 14:11)
   Need leads to God; Need all but teaches prayer.
   God casts the beaten rod in the fire,
   And punishes Assyria proud of his deed.
   He is wise who understands the work of God. (Isaiah 10:12)

Dye weelde werdrietich eyn laſtighe dracht
Miſbruckt gads gaue in luſt vnd pracht
Iuer ſott bowt den tōn van Babell
Men twiſt om twoort dat wert em fabell

So dwalt men in ſeedenn dor twiſt uit geeloof
Goot gyſt dat ricke lantt tot eyn rooff
Enn ſendt eyn Roede vredt enn hoichmoedich
Verderfft landt vnd luid mut Rouuers bludich

This series of prints shows the rise of a country to wealth and power, the misuse of those riches, God's punishment, and the resulting conversion and deliverance. Each of the four scenes is shown in a globe, a device also found in other prints in this book. (See NRS 20 and XXXI.) This image is used to convey the message that what one sees may seem fabricated; but it is, in fact, a reflection of real life. The artist of these prints was also the etcher of NRS 5 and 17.

The first print situates the action. Seated in the center of a town square is the richly dressed and crowned female personification of The Netherlands. A map on her lap gives a geographically more precise location, the coast of Flanders with the city of Antwerp on the river Scheldt. Until near the end of the 16th century Antwerp was the most important commercial city of the land. The Netherlands herself is surrounded by personifications of her cities and provinces: boys with city-crowns on their heads, all busily engaged in various trades and crafts. The milch cow on the left was to become a symbol of Netherlandish productivity. The resulting profits and riches are presented to her by the angelical figure of Fortune. The verses stress that the prosperity of the country derives from the favor and mercy of God.

The second scene shows the squandering of the earned wealth in worldly pleasures. The Netherlands, seated on her throne adorned with a peacock, and a handsome young man scatter on the ground coins which are eagerly gathered up by two young women. The clothed woman on the left is recognizable, by her mirror and headdress decorated with peacock feathers, as Pride. The naked woman on the right represents Intemperance; the grapes in her bowl and the spilled pitcher point to alcohol abuse, or perhaps wastefulness in a more general sense. On the right, three of the provinces or cities argue over biblical interpretation. The book in the center reads *gekijf om Gods woort* (quarrel about God's word). The province on the far right even goes so far as to consult a fool on his opinion.

In the third print, entitled the Evil World, the rich country is punished for her evil ways. God has sent his cruel and proud Rod to kill and lay waste to the land. In this print the instrument of punishment takes on the form of a warrior whose helmet ends in a birch rod, literally the Rod in God's hand. He is the King of Assyria described in Isaiah, 10: 5–6: "The Assyrian! He is the rod that I wield in my anger, and the staff of my wrath is in his hand. I send him against a godless nation, I bid him march against a people who rouse my wrath, to spoil and plunder at will and trample them down like mud in the streets." The scene is one of destruction. The Netherlands herself lies naked and bound on the ground, while around her her cities or provinces are slaughtered. She is tread upon by the Rod and a female figure; together they clutch a sword. This female figure is a personification of Violence or Destruction dressed in the lion skin of Hercules, clutching a human heart and accompanied by a wolf. In his left hand the Rod raises a bag of money, the spoils of his plundering of the rich lands.

In the fourth and final print The Netherlands, as a result of the punishment, has turned from her evil ways and has returned to God through prayer. God casts the Rod He had used into Hell, with a millstone around his neck. There he is eagerly awaited by the Devil and the Whore of Babylon. Meanwhile, The Netherlands is rewarded for its conversion with a crown from heaven.

Although few specifics are given, the sequence of events in this series can be seen as a religious interpretation of historical events. The awareness that the prosperity of The Netherlands was dependent upon the grace of God was absent in the land. Instead wealth was squandered in pleasure, while religious dispute led to fighting rather than to common Christian conduct of life. The killings and destruction which feature in the third illustration must reflect the war and religious persecution which raged in the late 1560s and early 1570s. The Rod surely can be identified as Alva. There are similarities in appearance with other portrayals (compare NRS 5 and 18) and other instances in which Alva is called "the rod of God." (See NR 7.) The adjectives "cruel" and "proud," used to describe the Rod, are common in other characterizations of Alva. The fourth scene would seem to express not so much the reality but the desired outcome. Here the message of the series as a whole becomes clear. To avert the violence of the war which God has brought upon the country as a just punishment for her sins, the people are called upon to disregard worldly pursuits and,

Noot dringt tot gott Noot lehrt bidden schir
Goot werpt de geslagen Roeid int swir
End strafft Assur stolt nha siner daet   Esai: 10
Hi is wys dye dyt werck gads verstaat

through prayer, to convert to a true Christian life. If this course of action is followed, then God will destroy the enemy, who after all is only an instrument in his hands.

The destruction of this instrument, the oppressor, is also the subject of an engraving *Punitio Tirannorum* (The Punishment of Tyranny) (NR XLIII) by Hendrick Goltzius, an image very similar to the fourth print in this series. It pictures the fall of the tyrant into the open Mouth of Hell, referring to Isaiah 14: 4–6: "See how the oppressor has met his end and his frenzy ceased! The Lord has broken the rod of the wicked, the scepter of the ruler who struck down peoples in his rage with unerring blows, who crushed nations in anger and persecuted them unceasingly." The crown of peacock feathers, the symbol of his pride, has fallen from his head, and his loss of power is indicated by the broken sword.

Unlike other prints this series does not ridicule the Spanish, call for revolt, or attempt to rally support for the Prince of Orange. Instead, it gives an explanation of current events and a solution, although the scenes remain allegorical. By drawing a parallel between the history of the Old Testament Israelites and the situation in which the Dutch found themselves, an empathy with Jewry developed which has marked Dutch history ever since.

XLIII. Hendrick Goltzius, *The Punishment of Tyranny*, 1578?

INSTRVMENTA SERVITVTIS ROMANAE

FIDEI ET LIBERTATIS CHRISTIANAE DEFENSORES POPVLIQ PASTORES

24

THE PONTIFICAL TIARA OF ROMAN TYRANNY
(IN THIARAM PONTIFICIAM TYRANNIDIS ROMANAE)

Maarten de Vos (1532–1603) (attributed to)
Drawing, ca 1580 with inscriptions added after 1605
41 x 54.8 cms
Stichting Atlas Van Stolk, Historisch Museum, Rotterdam

Literature: A.V.S. 343; K. en P. 69.
Willem van Oranje: Om vrijheid van geweten, nr B 16.

The focus in this drawing is the Whore of Babylon, used here as a symbol of the papacy, crowned with the "papal tiara of Roman tyranny." The drawing attacks the papacy by revealing its "true nature" and showing the consequences of her tyranny. Little strips of papers with explanatory inscriptions have been pasted onto the drawing. Examined closely and viewed in its broader historical context, the drawing yields a more intricate and more political message.

The basic compositional element is the contrasting of the two groups of rulers in the left and right foreground. On the left are those enslaved in the service of Rome. Chained to the papacy, this group is accompanied by members of the clergy who carry papal bulls. Their submission is accentuated by the fact that they have lost their crowns and scepters, which lie on the ground at their feet. In the upper left corner above this group the fury Injustice (*Inius*) flies with bat-like wings, a head of snakes, and wielding a sword and a torch. On the right are the free kings, rulers, and magistrates under God, defenders of freedom and the Christian faith. Appearing above this group is the angel Piety *(Pietas)*. She carries a laurel wreath and a palm leaf, signs of merit and victory. Between these two groups the bodies of fallen rulers lie on a heap. Kneeling at the feet of the Whore is Emperor Frederick Barbarossa. This German emperor was excommunicated by Pope Alexander III in 1160, and was not recognized again until he had humbled himself and had knelt down and kissed the feet of the pope in 1177. (See NRS IV and 14.)

The Pope's council is made up of a Brood of Vipers *(Progenies Viperina)*: snakes, a vulture, and a toad-like creature, all dressed like bishops and cardinals. In the background are several scenes of the so-called "Spanish Fury of Antwerp" of 1576, of a large execution carried on under the banner of the Spanish Inquisition, and of the Parisian slaughter of the French Huguenots during the Massacre of St Bartholomew's Night in 1572.

The drawing as described here would seem to offer a fairly conventional, though biting anti-Catholic image. However, when all the pasted-on inscriptions are taken into account a more specific interpretation can be considered. The inscription on the left, *Proditio Anglicana Sub Parlamento A Jesuitis Machinata,* is a reference to the so-called "Gunpowder Plot" of 5 November 1605, an assassination attempt on the English King James I and members of Parliament, allegedly inspired by Jesuits. This must result in

103

a date for the inscriptions in the period 1605–1610, while the drawing itself is several decennia older. It seems likely that these inscriptions were added to give an updated meaning to an old drawing.

In 1606 a stalemate between the warring parties in The Netherlands had been reached and both sides were considering negotiations for peace or a truce. Some of the most ardent opposition to an agreement came from the Calvinists in the Republic of the Northern Provinces. They wanted to continue the war against the Spanish, to spread Calvinism, and to liberate the Southern Provinces from the "Spanish Catholic Yoke." Seen against these circumstances, the drawing can be interpreted as a deploring of the enduring plight of the enslaved Southern Provinces, and an appeal to those provinces to throw off their fetters and join the liberated side. The inscription (a quotation from The Revelation 18: 4 and 6) borne by the angel on the right, calls upon the people to leave Babylon; likewise the free rulers beckon those in servitude toward their side. The cup borne by the Whore of Babylon bears the label *Philtrum Pacis* (the Potion of Peace). This presents a clear denunciation of the truce or peace treaty, which in the eyes of the Calvinists would ensure the continuation of enslavement and religious persecution.

25

LAMENT OVER THE DESOLATION OF THE NETHERLANDS (BELGICAE DELACERATAE LAMENTATIO)

Hans Collaert I (ca 1530–1581), after a drawing attributed to Ambrosius Francken (1544–1618)
Engraving, ca 1570–1580
36.2 x 46.5 cms
Stichting Atlas Van Stolk, Historisch Museum, Rotterdam
Literature: F.M. 520, A.V.S. 411, K. en P. 60.

Beclaghinge der Nederlantscher Verwoestinghe.	Lament over the Desolation of The Netherlands
O Nederlant waer sijdij toe ghecomen nu?	O Netherlands, what has become of you?
Swaer is u allende onverdraechlijck u verdriet	Heavy is your burden, unbearable your suffering.
Rijckdom, Schoonheid, eijlaes twort al benomen u	Wealth, Beauty, alas, all is taken from you.
Die ghij oijt meest trouwe beweest die en achten u niet	Those to whom you were most loyal, they do not respect you,
Want sij berooven u therte al soomen hier siet	For they steal your heart, as can be seen here.
Ja die u naest sijn helpen tot dees malitie.	Indeed, those who are nearest help in this crime.
En de vremde die u dienen (och dat sulcx geschiet)	And the foreigners who serve you (oh, how can it be)
Berooven u Cieraet bij foute van Justitie	Rob you of your Jewel, by lack of Justice.
Eerghiericheid en Eijgen baet toont haer conditie	Ambition and Greed display their nature.
Wantrouwe en Nijdicheid wilt elck doen den eet breken	Distrust and Envy cause all to break their vow,
Maer Getrouwicheid beletter veel sulcke vitie	But Loyalty prevents many from that mistake.
Die Godt betrout sal noch sien al sijn leet wreken.	Those who trust in God will have all avenged.

The engraving presents an allegorical view of the situation in The Netherlands in the 1570s. The personification *Belgica* is being raped and robbed by four Spanish soldiers. The inscription at the bottom of the print states that these crimes are being perpetrated by those to whom The Netherlands has always been most loyal. In the second verse the same are referred to as the "foreigners who serve you." Robbing, murdering, and pillaging Spanish soldiers are often the subject in propaganda prints, as in this case, where the print presents a more general lament on the war.

The "Spanish" army in The Netherlands consisted of only a minority of Spaniards. Most of the other soldiers were recruited from countries such as Germany, Austria, and The Netherlands itself. While the Spanish and Italian divisions were generally well-disciplined, mutiny among other ranks occured often. Payment was frequently overdue, which led the soldiers to seek alternative ways of reimbursement. These raids most often took place in the Southern Netherlands, in friendly territory where the soldiers were stationed for protection and defense against attacks from Orange's legions. The most infamous assault occurred in 1576 during the so-called "Spanish Fury" when more than 5000 soldiers rebelled and occupied the city of Antwerp. There they plundered, murdered, and robbed for months on end.

Perhaps the print was made after this massacre had taken place, although there are no specific references to the event. The small scenes in the background show the destruction of a castle and a small town, as well as a raid on a farm. The large ruin behind *Belgica* is a reminder of the former greatness which has now been destroyed. The rape of The Netherlands is being committed in the presence of two allegorical female figures, Ambition *(Ambitio)* and Greed *(Avaritia)*, who look on approvingly. They personify, in the first instance, the motives of the soldiers who commit the crime. On a more general level both are often cited as motives behind Alva's tyranny and behind Spain's oppression in general.

At the top the unity of the nation, represented by the shields of the seventeen provinces, is preserved by Loyalty *(Fiducia)*, despite the efforts of Distrust *(Diffidentia)* and Envy *(Invidia)* to break the chain. The verses at the bottom conclude with the assurance that all who place their trust in God will see their suffering avenged.

26
THE NETHERLANDS DELIVERED FROM THREE TYRANTS

Anonymous
Engraving, ca 1578–1579
22.9 x 31.8 cms
Stichting Atlas Van Stolk, Historisch Museum, Rotterdam
Literature: F.M. 795, A.V.S. 684.
Willem van Oranje: Om vrijheid van geweten, nr C 27.
W. Harms, *Deutsche illustrierte Flugblätter*, volume 2, pages 66–67, nr II–34.

O Nederlant nu van dry tirannen verlost syt
Den eersten met schanden wt den lande geweken
Dese twee met pestilentie geslagen in cortter tyt
Godt can tsynder tyt alle boosheyt wreken

Dus weest voorsichtich gebruyckt fortuna by maten siet
Op dat sy niet en misgonne u vryheyt vercregen
U weder en sette als voorleden in Iammer en verdriet
Onder tirannen gewelt daer ghy in hebt gelegen

O Netherlands, you are now delivered from three tyrants:
The first fled the country in shame,
The last two struck with pestilence in short time.
God can in his own time avenge all wickedness.

So be prudent and use Fortune with temperance.
Take care they do not begrudge you your newly won freedom,
And return you to the former state of misery, sorrow,
And tyrannical violence under which you once resided.

In the center of the print the Duke of Alva is depicted in a melancholy pose, flanked by two figures who symbolize his fate. The fool on the left holds a miniature version of Alva's statue in Antwerp, and the accompanying verse reminds the viewer that "Pride goes before a fall" and warns of tyrants who sing their own praise. The figure of Time serves as a reminder of the short time mortals (and especially Alva) have left on earth. The bodies of Don Juan and Requesens rest on their coffins which bear biblical passages referring to vanity and mortality.

In contrast to the fallen rulers, the upper half of the print praises the wise government of the Prince of Orange and Matthias, Archduke of Austria. Matthias was invited by the States General to assume the governorship of The Netherlands in 1577 after a conflict with Don Juan. Matthias resigned in 1581. Orange and Matthias are praised for wisdom, diligence, benevolence, and humility before God. Dignity and Virtue guide their rule. The jumping horse *Belga* represents the country's freedom.

On 1 October 1578 Don Juan of Austria, for only two years governor of The Netherlands, died of the plague in his army camp near Namen. He had succeeded Don Luis de Requesens y Zuñiga, who had been governor since Alva's departure. Sworn in on 29 November 1573, Requesens had reluctantly accepted Philip's request to fill the vacant position. After little more than two years Requesens succumbed to a fever on 5 March 1576. To the Dutch it was evident that the hand of God was at work. The disgraceful departure of Alva and the subsequent deaths of his two successors were interpreted as God's punishment for the cruel and unchristian rule of the Spanish oppressor. (See also NR XXXIV.) God was on their side, destroying their enemies.

In this context a verse in the print states:

Everyone in The Netherlands who loves truth
Should wisely live together in peace.
Your Spanish enemies, who bring you misery,
God has removed, driven from your paths.

EVANGE
LI.
IVRAMĒ
TVM.

Maeckt v op ghy bedroefde, Syt ghetroost vol trouwen.
Verquickt v, o Belgica van de perse vol rouwen.
Werdy nu verlost door een wijs Prince met vlijt.
Die tseemonster dooden sal dat veel Mans en Vrouwen
Sonder Reden vermoort heeft, om syn aighen profijt.
Maer alle quaet straft de heere tot sijnder tijdt.

Den waerachtighen Perceus vut liefden gheloedich.
Die Andromida verlost heeft van die tanden bloedich.
Sydy o Nassouwe tot vreucht van dese Landen.
Godts seeghen bewaerdt v in v saecke voorspoedich.
En brenght onsen vijandt Tseemonster tot schanden
Godt heeft alle macht alleen in sijn handen.

Op die Belofte ons Coninex door een vast tractaet.
Staen wy Landen op ons preuilegien met Raet.
Als Hertoghe van Brabant beuesticht met eenen eedt.
Om ons voor te staen maer den Ouden haet.
Socht ons te bederuen Godt is diet Weet.
De Leughen deckt haer, onder des Waerheijts cleedt.

27

THE SHIELD OF WISDOM
(DEN SCHILT DER WYSHEYT)

Hieronymus Wierix (1553?–1619) (attributed to), after a drawing attributed to Maarten de Vos (1532–1603)
Engraving, 1577–1580
Published by Pieter Baltens (?) (1525–1598)
32.8 x 40.8 cms
Stichting Atlas Van Stolk, Historisch Museum, Rotterdam

Literature: F.M.S. 588A, A.V.S. 461.
M. Mauquoy-Hendrickx, *Les Estampes des Wierix,* nr 1654.
Willem van Oranje: Om vrijheid van geweten, nr C 68.

Maeckt u op ghy bedroefde, Syt ghetroost vol trouwen
Verquickt u o *Belgica* van de persse vol rouwen
Werdy nu verlost door een wys Prince met vlyt
Die tseemonster dooden sal dat veel mans en vrouwen
Sonder reden vermoort heeft om syn ayghen profyt
Maer alle quaet straft de heere tot synder tydt

Den warachtighen Perceus wt liefden gheloedich
Die Andromida verlost heeft van die tanden bloedich
Sydy o Nassouwe tot vreucht van dese Landen
Goidts seeghen bewaerdt u in u saecke voorspoedich
En brenght onsen vyandt Tseemonster tot schanden
Godt heeft alle macht alleen in syn handen

Op die Belofte ons Conincx door een vast tractaet
Staen wy Landen op ons previlegien met Raet
Als Hertoghe van Brabant bevesticht met eenen eedt
Om ons voor te staen maer den Ouden haet
Socht ons te bederven Godt is diet weet
De Leughen deckt haer onder des Waerheyts cleedt

Restore yourself, sorrowful one, be consoled and confident.
Lift yourself, *Belgica,* from the mournful oppression.
Now you will be delivered by a wise and diligent prince
Who will kill the sea monster which has murdered
Without reason many men and women for its own profit;
But God punishes all wrong in due course.

The noble Perseus, who in his goodness
Rescued Andromeda from the bloody jaws,
Are you, Nassau, to the joy of these lands.
God's blessing protect you in your successful cause
And bring our enemy, the sea monster, to disgrace.
God alone has all power in his hands.

On the Promise by our King, laid down in a treaty,
We the Provinces rightfully stand by our Privileges.
As the Duke of Brabant, he has sworn
To stand by us, but the old hatred
Sought to ruin us, as God knows.
Falsehood conceals herself under the cloak of Truth.

The presentation of the print's political message in the form of a well-known and recognizable example or metaphor was an effective instrument in the hands of the designers of propaganda images. In addition to the advantage of creating an instantly recognizable and thus understandable image, it gave the image a measure of truth and inevitability, or irreversibility, as regards the situation's outcome.

The example used in this instance is the Greek legend of Perseus and Andromeda. According to Ovid's *Metamorphoses*, Andromeda, the daughter of Cephus and Cassiopeia, in an attempt to satisfy the god Poseidon, was chained to a rock and left to be devoured by the sea monster. The hero Perseus, however, killed the dragon, rescued Andromeda, and married her.

In this print, which is based on an anonymous drawing in Paris, the role of Andromeda is played by a female personification of the province Brabant. The sixteen other provinces are seated in the background, each identified by her shield. The sea monster which is about to devour Brabant is interpretable by several coats of arms as the Spanish Tyranny. The large coat of arms on the monster's back is that of Philip II; on its breast are the shields of the Duke of Alva and the Inquisition. Under its cloak are concealed several masked figures who personify Falsehood and Deceit. Willem of Orange features as the hero Perseus who comes to Andromeda's rescue. The Prince is armed with The Shield of Wisdom *(Den schilt der wysheyt)*, and his actions are being blessed by the hand of God, visible among the clouds above Orange. At the feet of Andromeda lie the remains of earlier victims of the Spanish Tyranny.

The conceit of the print can be traced to the year 1577 in which Willem of Orange, by invitation of the States General, was appointed *Ruwaard*, protector of Brabant. (The third verse refers to him as Duke of Brabant.) As a portion of the September 1577 festivities which accompanied Willem of Orange's entrance into Brussels, where the States General were assembled, a *tableau vivant* was performed portraying Willem as Perseus, the liberator of The Netherlands.

The account of the Prince's entry into Brussels by Jean Baptiste Houwaert contains a woodcut of this scene by Antonij van Leest (NR XLIV) which is clearly related to the engraving. Other *tableaux vivants*, performed at this occasion in honor of Willem and exemplary of his leadership, featured David with the head of Goliath and Moses delivering the Jews.

112

XLIV. Antonij van Leest,
Willem as Perseus, ca 1578

113

114

28

THE TRIUMPH OF PEACE

Wierix (attributed to one of the brothers), after Willem van Haecht I (active ca 1552–1577)
Engraving, 1577
Published by Pieter Baltens (1525–1598)
37.4 x 45.3 cms
Stichting Atlas Van Stolk, Historisch Museum, Rotterdam

Literature: F.M.S. 723B, A.V.S. 605a.
M. Mauquoy-Hendrickx, *Les Estampes des Wierix*, nr 1650–II.
Willem van Oranje: Om vrijheid van geweten, nr C 22.

Den godlijcken Peijs, veur de seventhien landen	The divine Peace for the seventeen provinces
Was traghe in haer compst, Door dese twee vijanden	Was slow in coming, because of these two enemies,
Dats den Ouden haet, en die Verblinde Eijghen baet	Which are: Old Hatred, and Blind Self-Interest;
Maer nu breect den stock in dwiel, tot hender schanden	But now the stick in the wheel breaks, to their disgrace,
Want liefde ment sterck voirts Trouwe houwt vast tractaet	Because love drives on strongly and Loyalty strengthens the treaty
Verbonden met des lants Staten, door wijsen raedt	Joined with the States, by wise decision.
En den Tijdt maect de gemeijnte met Reden stoudt	And Time rightly makes the community bold
Om Discoort te Verdempen in spijt van tfortsich saedt	To destroy Discord in spite of the violent seed.
Wijs is den Coninck die sijn lant in vreden houdt	Wise is the king who keeps his country in peace.

On 8 November 1576 a peace treaty was signed which came to be known as the Pacification of Ghent. The States General agreed to a peace that would restore the unity among the seventeen provinces and deal with future religious differences by negotiation. The States General, however, was not legally authorized to conclude such an agreement. Given the fact that the treaty was reached in the period between the death of the governor Requesens and before the arrival of his succesor Don Juan, the question was: "How would King Philip react to the treaty?" The final line of the verse expresses the hope for a positive decision from the King. On 12 February 1577 the Perpetual Edict, an agreement which ratified the Pacification of Ghent, was signed with the new governor Don Juan, in agreement with Philip II.

These treaties gave rise to optimism soon to be shattered but still evident in this print. Peace is seated on a triumphal chariot, accompanied by Agreement and with Charity at the reigns. The chariot is drawn by three mules which signify the slow pace at which peace was reached. Under its wheels the chariot crushes the male personification of Envy or Old Hatred *(Livor)* and also instruments of civil war. Self-Interest, a woman bearing stolen riches, attempts in vain to stop the progress of Peace. On the right side all the seventeen provinces of The Netherlands kneel to welcome the chariot of Peace.

The background illustrates the destruction of Discord *(Discordia)*, who is strangled in a tug-of-war between the forces of Violence *(Violentia)* and The People *(Populus)*, led by Reason *(Ratio)*. Meanwhile Time *(Tempus)* chases away the three furies Alecto, Tisiphone, and Megera. This and the previous print (NR 27) are part of a series of five prints, attributed to the Wierix brothers and published by Pieter Baltens. All are allegories on various aspects of the political situation in The Netherlands around the year 1577.

29

A DIALOG BETWEEN MAN AND RELIGION
(TSAMENSPREKINGHE DEN MENSCH EN RELIGIE)

Wierix (attributed to one of the brothers), after Maarten de Vos (1532–1603)
Engraving, ca 1576–1577
Published by Pieter Baltens (1525–1598)
32 x 24 cm
Stichting Atlas Van Stolk, Historisch Museum, Rotterdam
Literature: F.M.S. 723D, A.V.S. 607, K. en P. 107.
M. Mauquoy-Hendrickx, *Les Estampes des Wierix*, nr 1655.

Tsamensprekinghe den Mensch en Religie

MENSCH: Seght my Religie, vanden hoochsten geboren,
Ghy geestelyck ghebruyck van den heere vercoren
Warom is u hoot verciert met sterren schoone,
RELIGIE: Om dat ick u den wech, tot den hemel vertoone
MENSCH: Tis wonder dat ghy draecht sulcken verscheurde cleet,
RELIGIE: Dats om dat my sweerelts hooverdye verleet,
MENSCH: Tis scande, dat ghy staet, met u borsten naeckt,
RELIGIE: Ic begheer dat ghy myn Inwendighe liefde smaeckt,
MENSCH: Den boeck my dan Oorcont?
RELIGIE: dats myns vaders verbont
MENSCH: Steundy dan opt Cruys met lust?
RELIGIE: ia ick dat is myn rust,
MENSCH: En ghy hebt vleughels aen?
RELIGIE: Ick doent hert tot god opgaen
MENSCH: Waer by den toom geleken?
RELIGIE: men moet gramscap breken
MENSCH: Die ghy vertreet ist noot?
RELIGIE: Jaet want ick ben des doots doot
MENSCH: Doorloghe die ick hier sie u niet aen en gaet?
RELIGIE: Neent, maer geveynsde, doen onder myn decksel quaet
Beroovende my en den Coninck elck synen staet.

A Dialog between Man and Religion

MAN: Tell me, Religion, born of the highest,
Thou spiritual joy chosen by the Lord,
Why is your head adorned with bright stars?
RELIGION: Because I point you the way to heaven.
MAN: Strange that you wear such ragged garments.
RELIGION: That is because I pity the world's vanity.
MAN: It is a shame that you stand with your breasts naked.
RELIGION: I desire that you taste my internal love.
MAN: What is the meaning of the book?
RELIGION: It is my Father's covenant.
MAN: Do you lean on the cross eagerly?
RELIGION: Yes, it is my comfort.
MAN: And you bear wings?
RELIGION: I raise the heart to God.
MAN: And why the bridle?
RELIGION: I must hold back wrath.
MAN: Must you trample him?
RELIGION: Yes, for I am the death of death.
MAN: The war I see here does not concern you?
RELIGION: No, but the hypocritical do wrong in my name,
Stealing both my state and the King's.

This print, like NRS 27 and 28, was engraved sometime in the years 1576–1577, shortly after the signing of the Pacification of Ghent. The message of the print is delivered in the form of a dialog between Man and Religion in which the image is explained to the beholder. The large and powerful personification of Religion dominates the composition. She stands in the foreground of a landscape in which armies march and battles rage on land and at sea. In the distance on the left an imaginary city is devoured by flames. In front of this, Religion stands gracious and majestic, triumphant over Death, the skeleton trampled under her feet.

The details of Religion's appearance are explained in the dialog under the print. The open book in her right hand is titled *Evangelium Pacis*, the Message or Good News of Peace. In the text Religion replies that the book stands for God's covenant or law. Its title and context, however, also seem to point to the peace treaty.

In the dialog Man asks Religion if she is really the issue over which the war is fought. Her answer is negative: the warring parties abuse her name and bring about the destruction of the country and the true faith. The message of the print is primarily a religious one. Only under the guidance of true Religion can Man reach peace and victory over Death.

Bibliography

GENERAL BACKGROUND:

Gelderen, M. van, *The Political Thought of the Dutch Revolt, 1555–1590*, (Ideas in Context, volume 23), Cambridge, 1992.

Geyl, P., *The Revolt of The Netherlands, 1555–1609*, London, 1932. (Reprint: 1988; Original Dutch edition: *Geschiedenis van de Nederlandse Stam.*)

Parker, G., *The Dutch Revolt*, Ithaca, 1977. (Revised English edition: Harmondsworth, 1985; Dutch edition: *Van Beeldenstorm tot Bestand*, Haarlem, 1978.)

Rowen, H. H., ed., *The Low Countries in Early Modern Times*, New York, 1972.

BOOKS AND ARTICLES:

Bartsch, A., *Le Peintre Graveur Illustré. The Illustrated Bartsch*, ed. by W. L. Strauss, New York, 1978ff.

Becker, J., "Hochmut kommt vor dem Fall. Zum Standbild Alvas in der Zitadelle von Antwerpen, 1571-1574," *Simiolus* 5 (1971), pp. 75–115.

Becker, J., "Een tropheum zeer groot? Zu Marcus Gheeraerts Porträt von Willem van Oranje als St. Georg," *Bulletin van het Rijksmuseum* 34 1986), pp. 3–36.

Beresteyn, E. A. van, *Iconographie van Prins Willem I van Orange*, Haarlem, 1933.

Boon, K. G., ed., *The Netherlandish and German Drawings of the XVth and XVIth Centuries of the Frits Lugt Collection*, volume 1, Paris, 1992.

Decavele, J., *Eenheid en scheiding in de Nederlanden, 1555–1585*, (Centrum voor Kunst en Cultuur), Ghent, 1976.

Geurts, P. A. M., *De Nederlandse Opstand in de pamfletten, 1566–1584*, Nijmegen, 1956. (Reprint: Utrecht, 1978.)

Het Geuzenliedboek, naar de oude drukken uit de nalatenschap van Dr. E. T. Kuiper, published by Dr. P. Leendertz. Jr., Zutphen, 1924.

Grapperhaus, F. H. M., *Alva en de Tiende Penning*, Zutphen, 1982.

Groenhuis, G., "Calvinism and National Consciousness: the Dutch Republic as the New Israel," (Britain and The Netherlands, volume VII, *Church and State since the Reformation. Papers delivered to the Seventh Anglo-Dutch Historical Conference*, ed. by A. C. Duke and C. A. Tamse), The Hague, 1981, pp. 118–133.

Groenveld, S. et al, *De kogel door de kerk? De Opstand in de Nederlanden en de rol van de Unie van Utrecht, 1559-1609*, 2d edition, Zutphen, 1983.

Harms, W., *Die Sammlung der Herzog August Bibliothek in Wolfenbuttel*, volume 2, (Deutsche illustrierte Flugblätter des 16. und 17. Jahrhunderts), Munich, 1980.

Harms, W. and B. Rattay, *Illustrierte Flugblätter aus den Jahrhunderten der Reformation und der Glaubenskämpfe,* (Kunstsammlungen der Veste Coburg), Coburg, 1983.

Hendrix, L. and T. Vignau-Wilberg, *Mira calligraphiae monumenta. A Sixteenth-Century Calligraphic Manuscript inscribed by Georg Bocskay and illuminated by Joris Hoefnagel,* Malibu, 1992.

Henkel, A. and A. Schöne, *Emblemata, Handbuch zur Sinnbildkunst des XVI. und XVII. Jahrhunderts,* enlarged edition, Stuttgart, 1976.

Hofmann, W., ed., *Luther und die Folgen für die Kunst,* (Hamburger Kunsthalle), Hamburg, 1984.

Hollstein, F. W. H., *Dutch and Flemish Etchings, Engravings and Woodcuts, ca. 1450–1700,* Amsterdam, 1949ff.

Ketters en Papen onder Filips II. Het godsdienstig leven in de tweede helft van de 16de eeuw, 2nd edition, (Rijksmuseum Het Catharijneconvent), Utrecht, 1986.

Knuttel, W. P. C., *Catalogus van de pamfletten-verzameling berustende in de Koninklijke Bibliotheek,* volume 1, part 1, 1486–1620, The Hague, 1889. (Reprint: Utrecht, 1978.)

Maltby, W.S., *Alba. A Biography of Fernando Alvarez de Toledo, Third Duke of Alba, 1507–1582,* Berkeley, 1983.

Mauquoy-Hendrickx, M., *Les Estampes des Wierix,* 4 parts in 3 volumes, Brussels, 1978–1983.

Mout, N., "The Family of Love (Huis der Liefde) and the Dutch Revolt," Britain and The Netherlands, volume VII, pp.76–93.)

Muller, F., *De Nederlandsche Geschiedenis in platen. Beredeneerde beschrijving van Nederlandsche historieplaten, zinneprenten en historische kaarten,* 4 volumes, Amsterdam, 1863–1882.

Presser, J., *De Tachtigjarige Oorlog,* Amsterdam/Brussels, 1963.

Rijn, G. van, *Atlas Van Stolk, Katalogus der historie-, spot-, en zinneprenten betrekkelijk de Geschiedenis van Nederland, verzameld door A. Van Stolk,* volume 1, Amsterdam, 1895.

Roettig, P., *Reformation als Apokalypse. Die Holzschnitte von Matthias Gerung im Codex germanicus 6592 der Bayerischen Staatsbibliothek in München,* (Vestigia Bibliae, Jahrbuch des Deutschen Bibel-Archivs Hamburg, volume 11/12, 1989/1990), Bern, Berlin, etc., 1991.

Strauss, W. L., *Hendrick Goltzius, 1558–1617: The Complete Engravings and Woodcuts,* 2 volumes, New York, 1977.

Veldman, I. M., *De Wereld tussen goed en kwaad: Late prenten van Coornhert,* The Hague, 1990.

Vignau-Schuurman, T. A. G. W., *Die emblematischen Elemente im Werke Joris Hoefnagels,* (Leidse Kunsthistorische Reeks), 2 volumes, Leiden, 1969.

Voet, L., *Antwerp: The Golden Age. The Rise and Glory of the Metropolis in the Sixteenth Century,* Antwerp, 1973.

Wagenaar, J., *Vaderlandsche Historie,* volumes 5 and 6, Amsterdam, 1770.

Wieringa, F. et al, *Republiek tussen Vorsten: Oranje, Opstand, Vrijheid, Geloof,* Zutphen, 1984.

Willem van Oranje: Om vrijheid van geweten, (Rijksmuseum, Amsterdam), Amsterdam, 1984.

Zijp, R. P. et al, *Geloof en satire, anno 1600,* (Rijksmuseum Het Catharijneconvent), Utrecht, 1981.

✧

Images of Discord

WAS DESIGNED AND COMPOSED BY
DOUGLASS S. LIVINGSTON OF SUTTER HOUSE,
LITITZ, PENNSYLVANIA. THE TEXT IS SET IN
MONOTYPE BASKERVILLE WITH DISPLAY LINES
IN BASKERVILLE AND DOROVAR.

✧

TEXT AND COVER WERE PRINTED BY ACORN PRESS,
LANCASTER, PENNSYLVANIA, ON MOHAWK SUPERFINE
WHITE SMOOTH TEXT AND VINTAGE VELVET COVER,
RESPECTIVELY; BOUND BY BINDERY ASSOCIATES,
ALSO OF LANCASTER, PENNSYLVANIA.

Index

Index

✧

Images of Discord

WAS DESIGNED AND COMPOSED BY
DOUGLASS S. LIVINGSTON OF SUTTER HOUSE,
LITITZ, PENNSYLVANIA. THE TEXT IS SET IN
MONOTYPE BASKERVILLE WITH DISPLAY LINES
IN BASKERVILLE AND DOROVAR.

✧

TEXT AND COVER WERE PRINTED BY ACORN PRESS,
LANCASTER, PENNSYLVANIA, ON MOHAWK SUPERFINE
WHITE SMOOTH TEXT AND VINTAGE VELVET COVER,
RESPECTIVELY; BOUND BY BINDERY ASSOCIATES,
ALSO OF LANCASTER, PENNSYLVANIA.